A RAINBOW OVER NORTHERN FOOTHILLS OF THE SIERRA MADRE OCCIDENTAL

BEAKED YUCCA IN A ROCK-BOUND ARROYO, CUATRO CIENEGAS BASIN

A SWEEP OF SAND DUNES, WESTERN CHIHUAHUAN DESERT

THE 980-FOOT BASASEACHIC FALLS, NORTH OF BARRANCA DEL COBRE

GARAMBULLO CACTUS IN A LAVA FIELD EAST OF SAN LUIS POTOSI

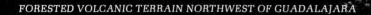

FORESTED VOLCANIC TERRAIN NORTHWEST OF GUADALAJARA

SUMMER-BLOOMING ORANGE CALTROP IN THE CHIHUAHUAN GRASSLANDS

TIME LIFE BOOKS

THE SIERRA MADRE

THE AMERICAN WILDERNESS/TIME-LIFE BOOKS/ALEXANDRIA, VIRGINIA

BY DONALD DALE JACKSON AND PETER WOOD
AND THE EDITORS OF TIME-LIFE BOOKS

WITH PHOTOGRAPHS BY DAN BUDNIK

Time-Life Books Inc.
is a wholly owned subsidiary of
TIME INCORPORATED

FOUNDER: Henry R. Luce 1898-1967

Editor-in-Chief: Hedley Donovan
Chairman of the Board: Andrew Heiskell
President: James R. Shepley
Vice Chairman: Roy E. Larsen
Corporate Editor: Ralph Graves

TIME-LIFE BOOKS INC.
MANAGING EDITOR: Jerry Korn
Executive Editor: David Maness
Assistant Managing Editors: Dale M. Brown,
Martin Mann
Art Director: Tom Suzuki
Chief of Research: David L. Harrison
Director of Photography: Melvin L. Scott
Planning Director: John Paul Porter
Senior Text Editors: William Frankel, Diana Hirsh
Assistant Art Director: Arnold C. Holeywell

CHAIRMAN: Joan D. Manley
President: John D. McSweeney
Executive Vice Presidents: Carl G. Jaeger (U.S. and
Canada), David J. Walsh (International)
Vice President and Secretary: Paul R. Stewart
Treasurer and General Manager: John Steven Maxwell
Business Manager: Peter G. Barnes
Sales Director: John L. Canova
Public Relations Director: Nicholas Benton
Personnel Director: Beatrice T. Dobie
Production Director: Herbert Sorkin
Consumer Affairs Director: Carol Flaumenhaft

THE AMERICAN WILDERNESS
Editorial Staff for The Sierra Madre:
EDITOR: Robert Morton
Text Editors: Marion Buhagiar,
Rosalind Stubenberg
Picture Editor: Jane D. Scholl
Designer: Charles Mikolaycak
Staff Writer: Carol Clingan
Chief Researcher: Martha T. Goolrick
Researchers: Peggy Bushong, Muriel Clarke,
Lea G. Gordon, Beatrice Hsia, Janice Pikey,
Editha Yango
Design Assistant: Vincent Lewis

EDITORIAL PRODUCTION
Production Editor: Douglas B. Graham
Operations Manager: Gennaro C. Esposito
Assistant Production Editor: Feliciano Madrid
Quality Director: Robert L. Young
Assistant Quality Director: James J. Cox
Associate: Serafino J. Cambareri
Copy Staff: Susan B. Galloway (chief),
Susan Tribich, Florence Keith, Celia Beattie
Picture Department: Dolores A. Littles,
Joan T. Lynch
Traffic: Barbara Buzan

CORRESPONDENTS: Elisabeth Kraemer (Bonn); Margot
Hapgood, Dorothy Bacon (London); Susan Jonas,
Lucy T. Voulgaris (New York); Maria Vincenza
Aloisi, Josephine du Brusle (Paris); Ann Natanson
(Rome). Valuable assistance was also provided by:
Bernard Diederich (Mexico City); Carolyn T.
Chubet (New York).

Editors' Note: Because the Sierra Madre is a great, sprawling region covering some 580,000 square miles of mountains and high deserts, this book has been written by two authors who visited the area separately. The first two chapters were written by Donald Dale Jackson; the last three and the Nature Walk were written by Peter Wood.

The Authors: Donald Dale Jackson, author of *Sagebrush Country* in The American Wilderness series, spent two months in Texas and Mexico hiking, camping and caving to gather material for *The Sierra Madre.* Formerly with LIFE magazine, he has written articles on sports and the outdoors and a book on American judges.

Peter Wood, formerly a staff writer for TIME-LIFE BOOKS and author of *Caribbean Isles* in this series, customarily divides his time between New York and the New England coast, where he is an enthusiastic small-boat sailor and skin diver. He forsook these pursuits for mountain climbing and desert probing in the Sierra Madre. Now freelancing, Wood has produced many magazine articles and a book on squash, a sport in which he has been a nationally ranked player.

The Photographer: Dan Budnik, a native of New York's Long Island, switched from painting to photography in the early 1950s; his first picture essay appeared in LIFE EN ESPAÑOL in 1956. Since then his work has been widely published and exhibited; ecology is a favorite subject. His photographs are featured in five other books in The American Wilderness series, as well as in a book about Rome in TIME-LIFE BOOKS' series, The Great Cities.

The Cover: Laid bare by erosion, the volcanic ribs of Mexico's great western range—the Sierra Madre Occidental—lie exposed in a 4,000-foot-deep cleft known as the Barranca del Cobre, or Copper Canyon. Abysses such as this one, whose flanks are gouged by small arroyos, are a striking characteristic of the Occidental. In the Sierra Madre Oriental to the east, erosion has carved lesser canyons from the limestone bedrock, and ground water has eaten out labyrinthine caves and pits more than 1,400 feet deep.

Contents

1/ Across the Río Grande 20
Gateway to the Sierra Madre 36
2/ The Dark Heart of a Cordillera 52
A Nature Walk in Cuatro Ciénegas Basin 68
3/ Where the Birds Are 84
A Glorious Botanical Confusion 104
4/ An Ocean of Mountains 118
Changing Face of the Desert 136
5/ The Barranca Country 148
Austere Beauty of a Far Place 166

Bibliography 180
Acknowledgments and Credits 181
Index 182

The Rough Embrace of the Sierra Madre

From the Big Bend country of Texas and the border of Arizona, the two great arms of Mexico's Sierra Madre —the Oriental on the east and the Occidental to the west—stretch down to Guadalajara and Mexico City, some 800 miles. Though pocketed with settlements, the two rough chains and the high desert basin between them encompass wilderness areas of extraordinary variety and grandeur. They include the unique gypsum dunes in the oasis at Cuatro Ciénegas (pages 68-82) and the cloud forest on the moist, Gulf-facing slopes of the Oriental south of Ciudad Victoria (pages 104-116), as well as the plunging barrancas that render some sections of the western range almost impassable.

On the map at left, national parks and forests, Indian reservations and public lands are indicated by red outlines; points of specific scenic interest, such as caves, are marked with black squares; mountain peaks are identified with black triangles. The notorious Comanche trail once used by Indians to raid in Mexico is shown as a dotted line. Desert areas are indicated with red dots and sand dunes are marked with patterned red dots.

1/ Across the Río Grande

Color was as extraordinary as form there — black, yellow, vermilion, white, brown, buff, all altered by distance and heat, all given mystery by every variation of light. PAUL HORGAN/ GREAT RIVER

I stood on a cactus-covered hill in the southeast corner of Big Bend National Park, Texas, and stared across the slender brown band of the Río Grande at Mexico. I could see a small farmhouse on the narrow floodplain and the treeless, white-walled village of Boquillas perhaps three miles downriver. Between the two was a rocky trail that climbed a hill behind the farm, then skirted the edge of a cliff. The trail was no more than 100 yards from where I stood. A red-tailed hawk flew a holding pattern high above the cliff.

In a few minutes two boys on a single burro came ambling up the trail, talking animatedly. I watched their slow progress until they vanished from sight. Then a man in a broad-brimmed hat and a white shirt came up the trail on foot with a boy. The boy would walk for a time, fall behind, then run at top speed until he caught up with the man, chattering all the while. I guessed that they were a farmer and son on their way to the village. I waited until the man saw me watching him and, feeling slightly foolish, I waved. He stopped for a few seconds, stared at me, then continued on without returning my wave.

Only a few hundred yards behind me on the American side, beyond a hilltop fringed with spindly ocotillo shrubs, was an elaborate trailer campground—paved in asphalt, carefully marked and sectioned off. It was equipped with rest rooms, water taps and small grills. Smoke curled up from the stove vents of a dozen large motor campers. Along the path I had taken up the hill there had been neatly printed signs that identified and described various plants.

It occurred to me, as I watched the Mexican's retreating back, that he and the trailer tourists could have changed places in 15 minutes, but each would have been bewildered in the other's world. The Río Grande at this point and at this time of year—December, the beginning of the dry season—was no more than a shallow stream, only about 25 yards across and maybe two and a half feet deep. But the cultural chasm separating the two societies on either side of the border was immense.

Yet the river is just an arbitrary boundary, a political rather than a physical border. Along this section, Río Grande seems very much a misnomer; there is nothing *grande* about it. It is simply a desert stream, easily forded. The landscape is essentially the same on both sides of it. Both sides belong to the same biotic province, that is, an area with plant and animal communities recognizably different from those of adjacent areas.

The geographers' name for this province is the Chihuahuan Desert. It is a vast stretch of land, reaching from the sagebrush country of the Southwestern United States to deep inside Mexico. Big Bend National Park is a part of the Chihuahuan Desert, and so are the northern extremities of the two great Mexican mountain ranges that were the ultimate destination on this journey of exploration: the Sierra Madre Oriental (Eastern) and the Sierra Madre Occidental (Western).

To most *norteamericanos*, mention of the Sierra Madre conjures up the treasure of gold that attracted Humphrey Bogart and his greedy pals in a celebrated Hollywood film. My motive for going to the Sierra Madre was considerably less complicated: I simply wanted to see a sprawling wilderness that the casual visitor never reaches. There are no tourist trailers in the heart of the Sierra Madre, no fancy hotels, very little English spoken. These reclusive mountains offer no easy welcome. But there is much to reward the stubborn intruder, including some of the most spectacular land forms in the Western Hemisphere.

Rising from the Chihuahuan Desert, the Occidental and Oriental ranges sweep southward in majestic parallel ramparts, jostling the clouds at altitudes of up to 12,000 feet for 775 miles in the west and 810 miles in the east. But it is not their snowy heights, nor their dramatic sweep, nor their peaks, strangely sculpted by erosion, that create the impression of grandiose scale. It is their breadth. Both the Occidental and the Oriental are so broad—each more than 100 miles across—that from the air they appear as endless wavy ranks fading into and beyond the horizon. Looking west through a pass in the Oriental, the traveler can see six or seven distinct ridge lines before the contours are lost to haze.

Close up, the Occidental and the Oriental differ markedly. The Occidental, born of volcanic upheaval, is more rugged, more austere. The Oriental, composed largely of limestone laid down by an ancient sea that once covered the region, is lusher and slightly more gentle. The differing origins of the ranges reveal themselves in some extraordinary interior features. The Occidental has stupendous waterfalls, one of which, Basaseáchic, plunges almost 1,000 feet. The Occidental also contains complex, steep-sided canyons called barrancas, some of which are undoubtedly deeper than the Grand Canyon of the Colorado, though no one has bothered to measure them.

The limestone of the Oriental is pocked with colossal, multichambered caves and, at various places where cave ceilings have collapsed, with the vertical open pits called *sótanos*. The word *sótano* is Spanish for basement, but the imagery is inadequate. The pits are of dizzying depths; some penetrate as far as 1,400 feet into the earth, deep enough to accommodate the Empire State Building.

The Oriental and the Occidental share one fascinating feature. Because of their sheer length, hundreds upon hundreds of miles through varying latitudes and temperatures, both ranges undergo radical transformations as they sweep south. In the north they are desert regions, sandy and dry, dotted with creosote bush and mesquite, yucca and ocotillo and a host of other plants that have made their peace with aridity. Farther south, where the ranges increase in altitude, their peaks and high draws are home to trees and wild flowers of the temperate zones. The ranges enter still another environment as they cross the Tropic of Cancer: a humid, thickly carpeted jungle of vines, tropical plants and the forms of animal life sustained by heavy rainfall.

Untamed and unyielding, Sierra Madre country is still an arena of human struggle. Hatchet-wielding woodcutters work the high pine forests; farmers cultivate isolated plots of coffee and other crops a day's climb from the nearest village. A simple fact of topography forces the agricultural Mexican up the mountainsides: only a third of Mexico's land is relatively level, and much of that is arid. The result, as the sociologist Nathan Whetten notes in *Rural Mexico,* is that "farming is practiced on hillsides so steep that it would be possible for a farmer to fall out of his field."

To a Mexican who draws his sustenance from this way of life, the

A morning sun lights the ramparts of the Chisos Mountains in Big Bend National Park, as the hills of Mexico lie in haze on the horizon.

name Sierra Madre—literally, mother range—must seem particularly apt. The origin of the name is, in fact, lost to history; one theory holds that it came from the way the Occidental and the Oriental, between them, cradle the country's high central plateau. Yet the same designation is given a third, smaller range far from the heartland—the Sierra Madre del Sur (Southern)—while, curiously, it is withheld from Mexico's highest mountains, the string of volcanoes that straddle the country horizontally just below Mexico City; presumably these peaks, 14,000 to 18,000 feet high, inspire more awe than simple filial respect. In any case, few Mexicans bother with the complexities of formal nomenclature. They call their ranges cordilleras, a word at once muscular and musical—and, to me, irresistibly inviting.

I decided on Big Bend National Park as the jumping-off point for my trip into the Sierra Madre precisely because it is a microcosm, a kind of concentrated miniature, of northern Mexico. The term miniature, to be sure, is only relative; Big Bend encompasses 708,221 acres, and is the seventh largest national park in the United States. Within its boundaries, desert and mountains combine in a stark and dramatic landscape whose hazards are hinted at in some of the admonitions in the park's guidebooks for visitors. Don't poke around with snakes, tarantulas and scorpions. Carry a first-aid kit, including tweezers to pluck out cactus spines. Be careful of washouts during the rainy season. If you become lost in the desert, arrange rocks every few miles to spell out HELP, with an arrow to show the direction you are headed in.

In fairness, it should be added that these admonitions appear in the guidebooks simply as sensible precautions to be taken in harsh country. For all the caveats, the appeal of the place is undeniable. The park's terrain sprawls and swoops, climbs and dives in myriad geometric patterns—domes, cliffs, mesas—with the Chisos Mountains in the center and the Río Grande on the west, south and east. The wide curve the river makes on its 107-mile course along the southern boundary is what gave Big Bend its name. But the dominant impression the park gives is of a mad collage of angular lines: the jagged peaks of the mountains, the V shapes of the canyons, the spiky stalks of the desert flora.

To an Easterner used to neat shrubs and clipped hedges, the park's vegetation seems to be forever reaching out, poking up, leaning off in weird directions—imparting an abstract beauty to the scene and at the same time an air of menace. Big Bend's thorny garden of plants tends to generate metaphorical excess, often in the realm of weaponry. Spine

The pencil-thin stalks of a candelilla plant, 15 to 20 inches in height, capture the sun's rays along a tranquil stretch of the Río Grande.

encrusted, bristly and tough, they remind a newcomer of lances, swords and daggers—sometimes all too vividly. Climbing a boulder in a Big Bend canyon shortly after sunset, I reached out for support and slapped my hand down firmly on the pad of a blind prickly pear. I spent the next three days gingerly plucking tiny brown barbs, called glochidia, from my protesting flesh. At that I was lucky; in grazing areas outside the park, cattle that include the blind prickly pear in their diet sometimes get a face full of glochidia, and are blinded as a result.

On another hike I leaned back to rest against a rock and brushed against a hedgehog cactus. I managed to get my hand between my skin and the hedgehog's spines before I made full contact, thus sacrificing one paw to carelessness. This time it took two weeks for the spines to work themselves out, but again I consoled myself that things could have been worse; the spines could have come from a lechuguilla. This variety of agave, found nowhere else in the world but the Chihuahuan Desert, is about as eye arresting as a plant can be. Out of a rosette of low-lying leaves it thrusts a narrow stalk as tall as 15 feet, topped when in bloom by red, orange, yellow or green flowers. But the leaves are tipped with spines so powerful that they can puncture a cowboy's thick boot or wound his horse. The agave lechuguilla is one of the main reasons why few of the park's horses have unscarred fetlocks.

Tender but wiser after my painful introduction to the arsenal of Big Bend's cacti, I turned my attention to a desert plant that appeared entirely innocuous—a perennial herb called candelilla, which looks something like asparagus and is very much at home on both sides of the Río Grande. It was a new species for me, and indeed harmless, but I soon learned that it generates a lot of trouble even so.

In Big Bend it is illegal merely to pick a candelilla, and in Mexico the federal government keeps a sharp eye on its growth. The reason is economic. To conserve moisture the candelilla stalks are coated with a wax that happens to be highly prized for use in shoe polish, chewing gum and floor wax. When the plant is ready for harvesting, it is pulled out of the ground whole and boiled in water with sulfuric acid added, whereupon the wax rises to the top and can be skimmed off. The operation requires very little equipment. While boating on the river one day I saw what local people call a wax factory, deserted for the winter, on the Mexican shore; it was no more than a series of cane-topped lean-tos huddled against a cliff. The wax fetches top prices in the United States; hence there is a temptation to smuggle it across—one kind of border traffic that nature cannot control.

In the end, what fascinated me most about the vegetation I saw was neither the cacti nor the candelillas but the profusion of grasses—chino and tobosa on the flats, bluestem and side-oats grama on the slopes. At first the sight of so much green comes as a shock to anyone accustomed to picturing desert terrain solely in terms of barren sands, baked dunes and dun colors. Then, belatedly, one recalls that by definition a desert is any place that generally averages less than 10 inches of rainfall each year. All manner of growing things can survive in such an environment—provided they have the ability, by one means or another, to conserve moisture.

The candelilla dons its waxy coat. Cacti hoard moisture in their spongy bodies. The ocotillo keeps water loss at a minimum by shedding its leaves in dry seasons. The yucca and the mesquite send down long roots to tap water sources deep in the earth. As for the grasses, their secret is the most elementary of all: they persist simply because they are hardy enough to endure extended periods of drought.

At Big Bend, as in most of the northern Sierra Madre, the rainfall is a feast-or-famine affair. In late summer and early fall, sudden and ferocious thunderstorms unload as much as an inch of rain in an hour, cloudbursts slash the parched earth into hundreds of washes, and even the scruffiest cacti bloom more profusely, brightening the landscape with splashes of purple and yellow and red. Then, for much of the winter and spring, there is no rain at all. December, the month of my visit, averages a mere half inch.

Exploring the park at this dry time, I was hard put to imagine it covered by a vast sea. Yet that was its condition, according to geologists' estimates, 100 million years ago. Great masses of limey sediments, composed of microscopic plankton and the ancestors of today's shellfish, were deposited in the sea. Then, gradually, the main body of water receded, leaving swamps filled with dense vegetation.

By 75 million years ago Big Bend had a whole new look. It was now covered with ferns, mosses and water-loving trees, and a haven for dinosaurs, enormous crocodile-like beasts and winged reptiles. These giant creatures prevailed for about five million years before they became extinct—possibly because of a drastic change in climate—and the small mammals that had coexisted with them began to proliferate.

Some 70 million years ago, the Big Bend area underwent yet another transformation wrought by a protracted process of mountain building. The layers of limestone that had been deposited in the ancient sea were upended, broken into blocks, curved into loops and otherwise re-arranged by uplifting, faulting and folding. Some 15 million years later, molten material from the earth's interior squeezed upward through the sedimentary rocks. Then further faulting and tilting tangled and in-terlocked the sedimentary and igneous rocks. An old Indian legend of-fers its own more romantic version of this process: when the Great Maker finished the earth and put stars in the sky and fish in the ocean, he had a big pile of rocks left over. He threw them all into one huge jum-ble and the result was Big Bend.

Through the millennia, rain and atmospheric gases have eaten away at the rocks. The intensity of the storms at Big Bend has helped to quick-en the pace of erosion, and so has the Río Grande. In ancient times the river's passage was a relatively easy matter of penetrating the softer clay sediments that covered the rocks; but as these sediments trapped the Río Grande in its channel, the river had to slice its way through hard rock. As it went it carved a number of spectacular canyons out of limestone mesas. At Mariscal Canyon, at the park's southernmost point, the rock walls rise to a height of 1,800 feet above the river. At Santa Elena Canyon, 35 miles to the northwest of Mariscal, the gap in the mesa looks like an enormous gate inexplicably left open in the middle of a gigantic stone fence, and in fact a 19th Century army officer named it Puerta Grande, Great Door.

Erosion and weathering at Big Bend have produced a dazzling va-riety of rock formations in rich hues of buff, deep brown, amber and lav-ender, and have also laid bare some of the park's primeval past. Embedded in rocks high on the Chisos peaks are the remains of pro-totypical snails, clams and oysters from the ancient sea. Though fossil hunting by amateurs is forbidden, paleontologists with special permis-sion to roam Big Bend have unearthed traces of many dinosaurs and, more recently, parts of three winged reptiles that lived at the same time as the dinosaurs, gliding through the air on batlike wings. The re-mains of two of these awesome creatures, called pterosaurs, were found in floodplain siltstone, those of the third in a sandstone outcropping. Measurement of the wings, neck and mandibles indicated that the pter-osaurs, when all in one piece, were 30 feet long and had wingspans of 50 feet—seven feet longer than the wings of a F-15A jet fighter.

In time, other wonders may be yielded up by Big Bend's rocks. Their exposure through erosion and weathering is, of course, a continuing process, and one that gives Big Bend a tantalizing look of incomplete-ness. Dwight Deal, a geologist who is general manager of the

Chihuahuan Desert Research Institute in Alpine, Texas, north of the park, says that geologists can spend their entire careers poking around in Big Bend without completely understanding its details. "I've been here for more than seven years," he says, "and I'm just beginning to learn enough about the particulars of the geological framework of this country to use it as an effective teaching tool."

Big Bend has, in fact, already seen service as a rocky classroom of sorts. In 1963 and 1964, moon-bound astronauts were sent to the park to study its rock formations and contours. After this basic grounding, they were better able to report back to NASA on the geology of the moon.

Long before the geologists and fossil hunters and astronauts, nameless nomadic Indians roamed Big Bend. One of their early encounters with the white man is memorialized at Lost Mine Peak in the Chisos Mountains. Some 16th Century Spanish explorers, the story goes, discovered gold on the mountain, took a number of the Indians prisoner, and forced them to work the mine. The Indians soon rebelled, and killed their captors; they then sealed the mine entrance to prevent further exploitation of their people. Though the location of the mine was later forgotten, a legend persists that if on Easter morning a searcher stands in the door of the chapel at Presidio San Vicente—an abandoned town on the Mexican side of the border—he will see the sun's first rays strike the exact mine entrance.

The first tribes to occupy Big Bend for more than brief periods were the Chisos and the Apache; ultimately the Apache drove out the Chisos and lived in the area until the 1880s. One of the last of the Apache was a chief named Alsate, who conducted frequent raids into Mexico and fought skirmishes with garrisons there. The Mexicans were never able to entrap him; he died, still eluding them, in a small cave on Pulliam Peak in the Chisos, not far from Lost Mine Peak. Another of Big Bend's enduring legends holds that when Alsate died, the contours of the mountain where he had made his last stand were suddenly transformed into an outline of the chief's defiant head.

But the real terrors of Big Bend—and of northern Mexico as well —were the nomadic Comanches. It had not taken the Comanches long to realize that the horse, reintroduced to North America by the conquistadors, would be of inestimable value to them in their travels around the plains of the southwest. Since horses were abundant in Mexico, the Comanches began crossing the Río Grande to steal them. The plunder continued, with some regularity, for more than 150 years until

Graceful tufts of needle grass turn russet as the fall dry season invades the Chisos Mountains in Big Bend National Park.

the mid-19th Century. By then the Comanches had a new reason to continue their forays across the border: the buffalo, upon which they depended heavily for food and other needs, was being systematically exterminated in the states. Every September large Comanche raiding parties would head across Big Bend, ford the Río Grande and gallop more than 500 miles south into Mexico, attacking ranches, stealing food and livestock and enslaving young Mexicans. The "Comanche moon" —September's full moon—signaled the start of the most dreaded time of the year for the Mexicans, and the pillaging lasted until November or December. The main Comanche trail, pitted by thousands of hoofs, was so clearly stamped on the Mexican land that it eventually became the border between the states of Chihuahua and Coahuila.

The United States Army finally subdued both Comanches and Apache in the late 19th Century, and cattle ranchers moved into Big Bend, there to remain until the establishment of the national park in 1944. One final flurry of violence took place in 1916, when the Mexican Revolution spilled across the river. A band of raiders attacked a small American garrison at Glenn Springs, some 10 miles inside the park's present southeastern boundary. They killed three men and a boy, and the United States cavalry promptly fortified the post. Its only signs today are neat borders of rocks along vanished pathways and tent sites.

I spent my last few days at Big Bend exploring the Chisos Mountains, which are related to the Sierra Madre Oriental. Both ranges, along with an intervening cordillera called the Sierra del Carmen that flanks Big Bend on the east and continues down into Mexico, are topographically part of a vast discontinuous chain that begins with the Rockies to the north. All were created during the same mountain-building period 40 to 70 million years ago. Today, almost all the way down this chain, many of the same life forms—animal as well as plant—recur, even though they are in enclaves hundreds of miles apart.

I had seen much of Big Bend's plant life, but little of its animals. Most of them are nocturnal, thus avoiding both the heat of day and predation by man and other animals. The park's most visible large mammal, if an extremely skittish one, is a subspecies of white-tailed deer. Big Bend is, in fact, the only United States habitat of this shy and delicate creature, though it also lives across the border in the Sierra del Carmen, and is called the Carmen Mountains whitetail. At 100 pounds, it is about one third the size of the desert mule deer, and an easy prey for a fellow occupant of Big Bend, the cougar. Known also as the mountain lion or puma and locally dubbed the panther, the cougar weighs up to 160 pounds. Only about half a dozen of these fierce, tawny beasts are reported each year in the park; their nocturnal habits, as well as a fear of their own worst enemy, man, keep sightings rare.

My companion on the trip into the Chisos was George Burdick, who teaches the children of park staff members during the school year and in summer works as a park naturalist, guiding visitors around. A particular favorite among the topics he discusses is Big Bend's wildlife, and I felt we were off to a good start when he expressed some cautious optimism about our chances of seeing one or two of its representatives.

Our first goal was a hidden canyon in the Chisos foothills, one of the few oases in the park that is verdant year-round. Our trail took us across shrub-dotted desert and then on an abrupt descent into a dry arroyo, where a single century plant bloomed in defiance of the season; it should have died in October, but the weather had stayed mild. As we moved up the arroyo, the vegetation thickened, a mass of prickly pear and sumac bushes and oak shrubs. Finally we heard the sweetest sound in the desert, the musical ripple of running water. A thin spray of water trickled down a tiered wall of rock perhaps 300 feet high; at the bottom was a dark pool about 100 feet around, draining in a shallow creek that flowed for only a few dozen yards before it was swallowed by thirsty shrubs. We paused at the pool and looked up at the rock wall; about halfway up we could see a tiny canyon wren, and a minute later we heard its song, starting high and plunging down the scale exactly as the water descended the rock.

Burdick checked the ground around the pool for tracks. "This is the only water in a pretty wide area," he said, "and there ought to be some customers here tonight—deer or javelina or maybe a bobcat. We probably won't see them but we might hear them." We moved back about 100 yards and took up watchful positions atop a rock. We sat in silence in the enveloping dusk, trying not to move.

The first stars winked above the soaring silhouettes of the mountains. I felt a chill: the temperature would dip below 40° F. that night, though in this part of the world that is considered relatively warm for December. Suddenly we heard a faint noise in the bushes, the sound of twigs and leaves being brushed. "Might be a ring-tailed cat," Burdick whispered. But it fell quiet again. I shifted position and instantly worried that the swishing of my nylon parka would scare off any animal. Then we heard another soft step on dry leaves, closer this time, and aimed our flashlights. A startled raccoon turned and bolted into a bush.

One of the five species of poisonous snakes at Big Bend, a black-tailed rattler flicks its tongue upon sensing an intruder. The snake's tongue aids its organs of smell by picking up chemical particles in the air and carrying them back to a set of unique sensory cells, located in the roof of the mouth, which transmits them to the brain.

Silence again. My ears were becoming attuned to it now, and I soon began to hear a series of faint brushing sounds. "Could be deer," Burdick said. But the sounds stopped. Maybe the deer sensed our presence, or maybe they were never there. Total animal count for the night: one raccoon. As we climbed down from our observation post and hiked back out of the canyon to our campsite, I asked Burdick about the ring-tailed cat he had mentioned. "A member of the raccoon family," he explained, "about the size of a half-grown house cat."

In the morning we headed into the higher reaches of the Chisos. Because of the altitude of the mountains, nearly 8,000 feet, they hold the few vestiges of the glacial age that survive in Big Bend. As the last ice age drew to an end, and the lower reaches of Big Bend warmed and dried out over the centuries, cold-climate trees such as ponderosa pine, cypress and quaking aspen gradually retreated to higher elevations. They remain there as oddities in an alien environment; seeing them, I found it hard to relate them to the desert vegetation flourishing below.

We climbed slowly up from the trail head in the Chisos Basin, an eroded bowl in the northwest part of the range, past splashes of red trumpetilla flowers and yellow damianitas. Both were blooming at least a month beyond their normal growing season in daytime temperatures of almost 70° F. Ahead of us, I suddenly saw my second animal of the trip: a stumpy piglike creature of about 50 pounds with a shiny black coat, waddling off the trail. "Javelina," Burdick said. "They're all over this country. You usually smell them before you see them." Their distinctive musky essence, he explained, is emitted from a gland near the tail whenever they sense danger.

Seeing a single javelina, it turned out, was unusual. More often they travel in bands of up to 25 or more. They wear a grumpy expression, possibly because of their pronounced nearsightedness, which may also be the reason they race off madly in all directions when frightened.

Farther up the trail we passed a drooping juniper, a tree common in the Sierra Madre Occidental but found outside Mexico only in the Chisos. The drooping juniper has such a hangdog demeanor that many visitors to Big Bend believe that it must be dying. A slim tree, it grows no higher than 25 feet, and has light yellow-green leaves that dangle loosely from its branches. But it is highly adaptable, growing as well on dry slopes as it does in wet canyon bottoms. Peering at us from a branch of the juniper was a gray-breasted blue jay known as the Mexican jay; it, too, has strayed from Mexico as far as the Chisos.

In time we reached a notch on the side of the mountain we were climbing, 6,900-foot Ward Mountain, and came in sight of a tidy little canyon not more than 100 yards wide and about 200 yards deep. Though it gave way to another, larger canyon on its far side, it appeared to be an entity in itself, a self-contained environment. No water was visible —springs are rare in this particular part of the Chisos—but vegetation was abundant: alligator juniper, so called from the checkered texture of its bark; piñon pine; stilted century plants; evergreen sumac; gray-green prickly pear; mountain mahogany and dozens of other plants.

I wondered aloud what the wildlife population of this curious enclave might include. "It would mostly be nocturnal," Burdick replied. "Coyotes and bobcats are probably around here at night, and there might be a bobcat den on the hillside." There was not enough prickly pear to attract many javelinas, he added, but there was a plentiful supply of deer browse.

"There's probably fifty different kinds of critters living in here," Burdick said. "Rock squirrels, cottontail rabbits, brush mice, spiny lizards. There'll be four or five kinds of snakes including a couple of rattlers in the summer. Ring-tailed cats. Skunks. You'll see this sort of wildlife community time and time again when you're in the northern Sierra Madre." What we saw now was a single cactus wren on an alligator juniper branch. The canyon was quiet except for the faint whooshing sound of the wind, and Burdick mused that canyons like this one might have been Indian camps as recently as a century ago.

We reached our own camp, an unmanned ranger cabin high in the mountains near Boot Spring, shortly before dusk and brewed up some freeze-dried stew for dinner. Then we went outside, and Burdick tried to summon up a coyote or bobcat with a plastic whistle-like caller.

While we waited, I asked Burdick if he had ever met a cougar in the Chisos. The closest he ever came, he said, was two years earlier, on the trail we had taken to Boot Spring. A group of park visitors had started off on horseback at eight one morning, and he had started hiking along the same route at 9:30. "I found cougar tracks on top of the horse tracks," he recalled, "I was that close." He lost the tracks and later found them again atop the ridge.

I must have looked a bit disappointed, for Burdick went on to tell me about two species, one animal, one plant, that I would be almost certain to see—if I revisited the park in the spring after my journey into Mexico. They were, he explained, two more examples of species found outside Mexico only in the Big Bend region. The plant is the pitahaya, or strawberry cactus; it blooms only from April to July, and produces a tan pod about two inches across, which peels like a banana to reveal a delicious fruit much like the one that gives it its nickname.

When the pitahaya begins to bloom, around mid-April, the other species Burdick had in mind arrives in Big Bend—the colima warbler. These birds were unknown outside Mexico until 1928, when one of them was spotted near Boot Spring. Sparrow-sized, gray and yellow, colima warblers winter in the Sierra Madre Oriental, then fly north to nest and breed in the Chisos. But they are not numerous, and every other May birders are invited to the Chisos to take a census. The first one, in 1967, totaled 92.

The evening passed with no takers for Burdick's caller: even the coyote proved elusive. Finally we conceded defeat, and turned in.

The next morning we took the South Rim trail, which offers a magnificent panoramic view of the park, the Río Grande, and a large slice of northern Mexico. The day was clear, and we were about 7,000 feet above sea level. Mountains, long ridges, buff-colored limestone cliffs and deep arroyos alternated in waves across the landscape. The terrain in the foreground resembled an enormous brown blanket with a dozen giant bobcats under it, bulging up in every imaginable shape. "It takes you three looks to see it," Burdick said. The Sierra del Carmen, blue and purple in the distance, dominated the view to the east. Santa Elena Canyon, one of the great canyons the Río Grande carved, lay 25 miles west. The river itself, 16 miles south of us, was a barely discernible ribbon of silver. Beyond it, on the horizon, the faint outlines of the first mountains of my next stop on this journey of exploration, the Sierra Madre Oriental, were visible through our binoculars.

Gateway to the Sierra Madre

For most of its 1,248-mile course as the border between Mexico and the United States, the Río Grande meanders quietly across sere deserts and gravelly grasslands that sweep away south to the Sierra Madre. About a third of the way in its journey to the Gulf of Mexico, however, the river abruptly plunges into a series of rocky defiles such as Santa Elena Canyon (right), whose walls rise 700 to 1,800 feet, quickening the river's pace and shutting out all but the noonday sun. There, at the southwest corner of Big Bend, the river is at its most intriguing, a waterway of varied moods and stark beauty.

The seasons contribute to the river's inconstancy. In late summer the Río Grande—or Río Bravo, as it is known in Mexico—lives up to its name. Though the area gets only about eight inches of rain each year, nearly three quarters of that falls from June through September. At this time the river may rise as much as 16 feet, although since 1914 its flow has been partially controlled by dams on the tributary Río Conchos, which drains part of the Sierra Madre Occidental and empties into the Río Grande from the south.

Swollen by summer rains, the Río Grande overflows its banks, ripping up miles of cane and reeds, rampaging through the canyons, and inundating enormous boulders that block the channel during the dry months (pages 46-47). Flash floods, roaring down from the mesas that line the river, surge unimpeded over the rock-strewn ground, stripping away the earth from beneath mesquite trees and other scrubby vegetation.

In the late fall—when the photographs on the following pages were made—the river shrinks down to more modest proportions, trickling over its rocky bed. Now reduced to an average depth of only about three feet, the water exposes sandy beaches and gravel bars that spread out as neatly as the surface of a suburban driveway. At this time, too, the remnant moisture of the recent rainy season finds a colorful expression in the still-blossoming riverside plants —salt cedar, esperanza and paper flowers. And the trickle of water through side canyons tops up the natural pools called tinajas that will serve as watering holes for animals over many months of drought.

This is an ideal time to view the river, for the evidence of its former violence is fully exposed to view. And yet its quiet side, the still beauty of the place, stands revealed.

Just inside the entrance to Santa Elena Canyon, the Río Grande glides between massive limestone walls composed of sediment laid down here millions of years ago when the whole region lay beneath a prehistoric sea. This type of sedimentary rock extends all the way south into the Sierra Madre Oriental.

The zigzag path of Santa Elena Canyon, beginning at the entrance cleft into the bluff (near left), cuts through a plateau of limestone known as Mesa de Anguila on the Texan side (foreground) and as Sierra Ponce in Mexico.

The ragged remnant of a stone wall, built as a simple water-control device, stands atop an arid mesa near a canyon rim of the Río Grande. The wall, flanked by spiky torrey yuccas and the pads of a prickly-pear cactus, was probably erected by local Indians to divert runoff from infrequent rains.

A deep pothole, or tinaja, in the floor of a narrow side canyon holds water left from the rainy season. Tinajas result if waterborne pebbles collect in a depression in a rock over which runoff periodically flows; after a long time swirling around in the runoff, the pebbles grind out a hole.

A tough, old mesquite tree (left) clings to the earth wall of a Río Grande side canyon. Runoff surging through the arroyo has exposed some of the roots without managing to dislodge the tree. A tenacious survivor in the dry land along the river and south into the Sierra Madre, the mesquite sometimes sends down taproots as deep as 100 feet in search of ground water.

At low ebb in November, the Río Grande (right) roils around an exposed gravel bar. Less than three feet deep and only about 60 feet wide at this point, the river swells threefold during summer floods, when it will bear most of these rocks farther downstream.

A quiet vestige of the river's power, this beach at the base of a buttressed canyon wall is formed of rock particles from the area. During summer rains, sediment washes down from the uplands, eventually to be deposited along the shore as the flood recedes. The next flood may wash it away.

A maze of broken carrizo, a reed that grows along the Río Grande, lies where floodwaters have deposited it on a ledge above the river. Left to dry in the desert air, such mounds of carrizo may remain for years as the sign of a particularly rainy season that swelled the river to an unusual high.

The Rockslide, a quarter-mile-long labyrinth of limestone boulders sheared off from the Mexican side of Santa Elena Canyon, constricts the flow of the river at low water. Dimples on the boulders' surfaces record the chipping action of rocks that are swept along by the river when it is in flood.

A salt-cedar bush swells with blooms in the late-autumn sunshine at the foot of a canyon cliff. A member of the desert-loving tamarisk family, the salt cedar readily takes root in thin, sandy soil near streams and rivers, where it crowds out most other plants.

The trumpet-shaped flowers of an esperanza brighten a canyon slope 80 feet above the Río Grande. Found as far south as Argentina, the plant grows in many places in the Sierra Madre and adjacent desert regions. Here it is near the northern end of its range.

The gleaming thread of the Río Grande, seen below the horizon from a point about three miles inside Mexico at the edge of Sierra Madre

country, snakes across a rocky landscape spotted with clumps of chino grama grass, prickly-pear cactus and yellow paper flowers.

2/ The Dark Heart of a Cordillera

These men dared to descend to a region where the whole of nature is reversed.   SENECA/ *QUESTIONS OF NATURE*

Ten feet inside the cave entrance, I waited a long minute to let my eyes adjust to the dark. I was near the top of a talus slope that fell about 100 feet to the floor of the most enormous room I had ever been in. Several little cones of light moved eerily across the floor. The lights, faint and filmy, as if they were underwater, came from the carbide lamps carried by the vanguard of our eight-member party. They appeared to be drifting through some surrealistic nether world, without perspective or norms of measurement.

Dwight Deal nudged me and we started down the slope. For the entire previous day, Deal had been telling me about this cave called Gruta del Palmito, 75 miles northwest of the city of Monterrey in the Sierra Madre Oriental. But the fact of it so transcended my imaginings that I felt vaguely embarrassed. I normally subtract 25 per cent from any superlative I hear, on principle; in this case such skepticism seemed shamefully small-minded. "Cave explorers talk about the Sierra Madre Oriental with the same wild glow in their eyes that mountaineers have when they mention the Himalayas," Deal had said. "For a noncaver like you to begin with Gruta del Palmito. . . ." He searched for an analogy. "It's, well, it's like doing your first climb on Kanchenjunga."

Nevertheless, there I was, just inside the cave now, struggling with the presence of this vast and dark chamber and trying to perceive its limits. But even though my eyes were adjusting and the light of my own carbide lamp punched the blackness, I could not see how far the room extended in any direction. Deal had given me the dimensions —150 feet wide, 525 feet long, 100 feet high—but numbers can be feeble tools of communication. The analogies I tried were not much better. I thought of the largest rooms I had ever seen—a cathedral in Italy, a dirigible hangar in California. But this room was something apart, its scope beyond my experience. And it was just the entrance chamber. The main room well beyond turned out to be the same height, but ranging from 200 to 400 feet in width and a full 1,600 feet long. The depth of the cave, from the entrance to its lowest point, is 667 feet.

There was another element about the cave that was new and strange —the sense of disorientation it gave me. I learned later that this is an emotion experienced by all first-time cave explorers. It soon passes, I was told, and one begins to feel more or less at home, but it stayed with me for the duration of my underground ventures in the Sierra Madre Oriental. It is as if your sensory perceptions are no longer reliable: you don't see quite as well, the things you touch don't have the texture you expect, sound is distorted, you're not altogether certain where you're putting your feet.

Gruta del Palmito—in English, Grotto of the Little Palm—derives its name from a small scruffy tree at the cave entrance. The Gruta region is an object of study for the Chihuahuan Desert Research Institute, which Dwight Deal runs. The institute has a broad charter to examine geological, zoological, botanical, archeological and other scientific aspects of the desert throughout north-central Mexico. As it happens, the Sierra Madre Oriental is one of the world's most spectacular areas of caverns and pits. Deal and other veteran cavers regard all these holes in the earth as caves—both those that can be walked into and those that must be descended by rope—and they estimate that there are more than 500 known caves in the Oriental. Deal assured me that an excursion to some of them would be rewarding both as unalloyed adventure and as a study of what he called underground plumbing, the system of water-carved passages inside the mountains.

My first view of the Oriental had been a glimpse of its northernmost foothills from the South Rim trail of Big Bend. A few days before my descent into Gruta del Palmito, I took a closer look at the entire northern part of the range from a small plane. North of Monterrey the Oriental is a series of discontinuous mountains, 5,000 to 8,000 feet high. The climate is arid in the lowlands of this region, and the most common plants are the same dry-country species that thrive in Big Bend

—prickly pear, lechuguilla, creosote bush, yucca, ocotillo, mesquite. Some of the same animals that tenant Big Bend—coyote, bobcat and cougar—patrol the washes and the tan hills.

Around Monterrey the look of the Oriental changes. The mountains rise dramatically, jutting up in a great wall to the west and south of the city. Just as dramatically, the range broadens here, spreading westward in a 100-mile-wide succession of ridges. When I asked one Mexican friend in Monterrey where a particular mountain was, he pointed vaguely toward the west and replied, "Seven ridges from here." Though towns and villages dot the range, some are reachable only by burro.

The Oriental varies as much from east to west as it does from north to south. The westernmost slopes rise more gently, almost imperceptibly, from the Chihuahuan Desert. Farther to the east the dominant sandy desert hues begin to give way to light green scrub and, still farther, to dark green; here pine forests start to crowd the ridges and mountaintops. The eastern flank of the range, less than 200 miles from the Gulf of Mexico, forms a steep escarpment, the antithesis of the gentle western slopes. Its pine forests, nourished by the precipitation that is borne in from the gulf by the prevailing northeast trade winds, are the richest green of all.

The real fascination of the Oriental, however, lies underground. Most of the range is composed of limestone, a soluble rock originally deposited as marine sediment—shells, coral and the remains of other sea life and masses of inorganic lime mud. The most porous and most easily dissolved variety of limestone, reef rock, abounds in the Sierra Madre Oriental, along with other kinds that are vulnerable to water action only along weaknesses such as fractures, fissures and spaces between grains in the rock.

Rain seeks out these weaknesses and attacks with a modest but highly effective arsenal of chemicals. As rain water falls, it picks up some carbon dioxide from the air and much more from decaying vegetable and animal matter in the soil it passes through. By the time the rain seeps into the limestone below it has become a weak solution of carbonic acid; but weak as it is, it has the power to dissolve the limestone, leaving water-filled holes and—once they are drained—the roofed caves as well as the deep open pits that local Mexicans and most scientists call *sótanos*.

Ultimately, the rain plus limestone plus tropical warmth have combined in the Oriental to produce an intriguing kind of jumbled topography known as karst, after an Adriatic region where it is also prominent. In a karst region the terrain, predominantly limestone, is riddled with sinkholes and other signs of collapsed surface; and since almost all water in such country drains away underground, rivers and streams are notably absent.

In the southern Oriental, karst is still forming. This part of the range lies below the Tropic of Cancer, where temperatures are high; moreover, rainfall is abundant—up to 100 inches annually in some places —since the range at this point is only 75 miles from the Gulf of Mexico. The northern Oriental was once as warm and wet as the southern Oriental, but global climatic changes have left it much drier, and its karst landscape has been worn down by surface erosion. But the north still contains relict caves such as Gruta del Palmito, which lured me underground for the first time.

Deal and I moved carefully down the talus slope until we reached the bottom of the entrance chamber. The floor was littered with dozens of huge, squarish boulders, some about 20 by 40 feet, which cavers call breakdown—chunks that have broken off the ceiling or walls along fractures that were created as the dissolving limestone weakened. Shiny, round little rocks, ranging from the size of a pea to one foot in diameter, glistened between the boulders. "Those are cave pearls," Deal said. He explained that as water seeps down through the cave's limestone, it becomes heavily laden with calcite, limestone's main component. Relentless dripping over the years creates basin-like depressions in the cave floor. Calcite sticks to fine grains of sand from the cave floor that have collected in the basins. Once the pearls form, further dripping rolls them around until they are smooth and highly polished, usually a lustrous pinkish white.

We caught up with the rest of our group and headed for the far side of the chamber. We were an odd assortment—a printer, a landscaper, a bookkeeper, two students, an archeologist, a geologist (Deal) and me. Most were Texans who had driven much of the previous night to get in a weekend of cave exploring, an avocation they pursue with the disciplined ardor of religious novitiates.

We made our way along a wall whose vertical, reddish-brown stripes made it look like a huge, rippled curtain of bacon; the color, Deal said, came from a mineral, iron oxide, that had been dissolved in water and precipitated out. Beyond the wall a passageway led toward another high-ceilinged chamber. I was trying very hard to retain a sense of direction, distance and proportion, but I felt myself losing it as we weaved past boulders, through rock tunnels, and in and out of alcoves where ceilings and walls were sometimes close enough to see, sometimes lost in the shadows.

Calcite was evident here, too. Stalactites hung like icicles from the ceilings and their companion structures, stalagmites, poked up from the floors. Where they met they formed columns, each of them one more obstacle to get around. In cave parlance such formations are called decorations; these happened to be a waxy white, though as we moved deeper into the cave we were to see them in far brighter colors and ever more fanciful shapes.

The footing was often slippery, sometimes steep. My hard hat rode unsteadily on a head unaccustomed to cover, and I was perspiring freely. The temperature in the cave was perhaps 75° F., about 20° warmer than it was outside, and humid; because rock is a good insulator, cave temperatures are not usually subject to surface variations, remaining constant year round.

We still had a way to go to reach the cave's main chamber. The approach to it began at a ledge in which earlier cavers had cut steps. The ledge is known as Paso de Muerte—Pass of Death—because of its perils. It is only a foot wide; on one side of it is a wall, on the other side a pit about 100 feet deep. I leaned into the wall and made my way across. Someone in our party had mentioned that children from the nearby village of Bustamante make a torch-lit pilgrimage every year to an altar deep in the cave's interior. I envisioned this column of little torchbearers stepping carefully across the Paso de Muerte, surrounded by eerie stalactites and stalagmites, and thought to myself that the scene might well fit in a Fellini movie.

Beyond the ledge lay a long breakdown slope—an obstacle course of more huge boulders—that fell away into borderless darkness. The slope dropped 325 feet, nearly half of the cave's total depth, at an angle of 30°, and our carbide lamps illuminated only part of the way down. After I descended about 100 feet, I could not help thinking about the return climb back up.

There was something else that was beginning to bother me. Here and there I had already noticed some distinctly unattractive signs of man's presence in the cave, such as graffiti scratched on the walls. Worse yet, I had seen some of the cave's delicate formations broken off, obviously by hand. I commented to one of my companions about the defacement. He nodded angrily, and said that even though the government's permission is required to enter this cave or any other

An icicle-like formation of calcium carbonate decorates a wall inside the cave complex called Gruta del Palmito. The dazzling white mineral is precipitated out of water seeping through the limestone bedrock. The rust color of the wall is caused by iron-bearing deposits in the limestone.

cave in Mexico, vandalism continues to be a problem. It struck me as a deplorable way to treat a national treasure like Gruta del Palmito.

Fortunately, some of the more inaccessible areas of the cave have escaped unscathed. At one point, a few of us made our way through a low passage into a room about four feet high, small enough for our combined lights to fill it. Since few people had been in this room, only an occasional footprint marred its pristine beauty. The ceiling was a maze of forms of every imaginable shape, in colors ranging from white to gold and orange to reddish brown. Delicate butterscotch-and-white calcite icicles hung from it, interspersed with long, hollow tubes that cavers call soda straws. There were also chunks of hanging rock that looked like carrots, pineapples and cornhusks bunched together, and a tangled mass of white rock that resembled the underside of a desert shrub, its roots grasping thirstily in all directions. Slender elegant columns reached from floor to ceiling. I thought of the term cave decorations, and decided that it was something of an understatement.

In another alcove, the sight was equally breathtaking. Only one of our party had been in this room before; the others, myself included, stared openmouthed at a succession of elegant little crystal formations on the wall: tiny, glassy needles called crystal points, projecting from orange-colored, velvety-looking flowstone. Somebody was reminded of a coral-reef formation, and the image did not seem at all farfetched.

As we emerged from the alcove, we found other members of our party staring up at a nearly vertical side wall. Ron Ralph, the archeologist, had started to climb the cave wall to see if there was an upper-level chamber. Finding none, he got stuck on his way down about 20 feet above the floor. He was having difficulty seeing the natural handholds and footholds he had used on his ascent, and the other cavers were talking him down.

"There's a good handhold about ten inches down from your left hand, Ron. . . ." Ralph lowered the hand, probing with his fingers. "I can't get the angle of it," he said. "Okay, okay," another caver said. "There's a foothold just down to the right of your right foot." Ralph found it, then moved his left hand to the lower hold. "What do I do now?" he said.

"Scream and jump," a caver joked. Ralph laughed; then his carbide lamp went out. Deal moved closer and aimed his light upward. "This is the only way to help a caver," the man next to me whispered. "You can't catch him if he falls, and if you try to break his fall you wind up with two injured instead of one. He has to get down himself."

As it turned out, Ralph—an experienced rock climber as well as caver—was never in serious danger of falling. He made it down in another minute, jumping the last few feet. He brushed himself off and smiled self-consciously. "Sorry, folks," he said.

We continued on down the long breakdown slope, scrambling from boulder to boulder and skidding every so often on slippery rocks. At the bottom we wound through several stalactite-stalagmite columns until we dropped down still another slope, a small one—and there, before us, was the vast main room of Gruta del Palmito.

Like the entrance hall, it was too big to see all at once; its edges blurred into blackness. The villagers of Bustamante had placed their altar at one end of this room. A hand-hewn wooden table and several icons were set in front of a 40-foot-high curtain of white flowstone, another calcite formation of surpassing beauty; it looked like a limestone version of a lava flow. As we stood there admiring it, our voices sounded thin and reedy in the void.

There was one more objective to be reached, and we crossed to the far end of the room. At the base of a high wall was a hole that seemed to me to be barely wide enough for a cocker spaniel to get through. Beyond it a kind of chute about 30 feet long dropped down under a low ceiling. I watched as the first members of our party began to maneuver through the hole, slanting their shoulders and moving one part of the body at a time. My confidence, which had regained some lost ground on the downhill scramble, started to slip away again.

Then it was my turn. I took off my hat and my day pack and launched myself head first into the hole. My shoulders made it through all right, but sections to the south kept getting stuck. Each time I strained and wiggled and got free, I felt my pants slide lower down my hips. I demolished a ball-point pen in my pants pocket and ripped a good wool shirt. Toward the end of the crawl way I found myself wriggling along on my back with my feet on the ceiling; for some reason I made better progress that way. At last I emerged, dusty, half-dressed and somersaulting, to the amused approval of my companions. I felt as though I had passed a formidable initiation rite.

We were now in the deepest chamber in the cave, more than 2,000 feet from the entrance. The room was the size of a tennis court, with a low ceiling, sloping floor, and orange flowstone walls. We stayed there until someone looked at his wrist watch and discovered that it was past three o'clock. We still had a three-hour trek to get back out of the cave—starting with the crawl way. "Just remember," Deal said, "if you get stuck, the rest of us behind you are stuck too." I got back through, this time the only casualty a pin in my watch.

On the long climb back I kept thinking about that crawl way, and it occurred to me that the apprehension I had felt was not so much a fear I would not make it as a fear I might *think* I could not make it. The thought was more alarming than the reality. Caves seem to touch some buried impulse in all of us. Perhaps they strum an atavistic chord that our conscious mind cannot hear. Almost everyone has some interest in caves, feels some attraction to them and yet some revulsion. Perhaps this ambivalence had been at the root of my sense of uneasiness upon entering the cave. Still, for all my concern, the slippery footing, the fear of fear itself, by the time I emerged I felt that this had been one of the supremely satisfying days of my life.

As I caught my breath outside Gruta del Palmito, I realized belatedly that something had been missing. I knew that caves harbor an astonishing variety of life; James Reddell, a Texas biologist, estimates that there are approximately 1,500 different species of cave fauna in Mexico alone. Yet I had seen none inside the cave. My companions explained that Gruta del Palmito is not noted for its fauna, and that the life that does exist there is so minute I would have had to hunt long and carefully to see it. Small frogs dwell in the ferns and lichens at the entrance; within the dark zone that begins 50 to 100 feet inside the cave, there are spiders, millipedes, beetles, daddy longlegs, and camel crickets—wingless crickets that live only in caves and other damp, dark places. But certain other typical cave denizens seem to be absent—blind cave fish, crayfish, snails and salamanders. The most conspicuous absentee is the commonest cave creature of Mexico, the bat.

I was to have better luck, at least so far as the bats were concerned, one afternoon a few days later in another cave, a small one near Linares south of Monterrey. I went there accompanied by a young Mexican biology instructor specifically to see a species of bat that I had previously met only in horror tales—the vampire. This cave marks the northern limit of the species, which ranges all the way southward to central Argentina and central Chile.

As we approached the entrance, my companion anticipated the question he knew I was bound to ask—about the vampire's notorious penchant for drinking blood. Quite true, he said. The creatures sleep during the day, then fan out shortly after dark to feed on the blood of burros, cows, dogs, horses and other animals. They approach their prey stealthily, alight and, as deftly as surgeons, remove a microscopically thin slice of skin with their razor-sharp incisors. As blood oozes up to the surface of the wound the vampire sucks it in, as through a straw, via a pair of grooves in the tongue. The victim, usually sleeping, rarely awakens as the bat drinks its fill.

The adult vampire, which weighs no more than an ounce and a half, consumes its weight in blood every 24 hours. The open wound it inflicts may look frightening, since such wounds clot more slowly than stablike punctures, but the excision is not painful and the amount of blood lost minor. The danger lies in the diseases the vampires transmit: murrina, a blood parasite deadly to cattle and horses; and the universally feared killer of animals and humans, rabies.

Inside the cave, we stepped around pools of guano that smelled strongly of ammonia, and pointed our flashlights at the ceiling, from which emanated a chorus of chittering squeaks. The light revealed a mass of about 200 vampires clustered in a recess in the domelike ceiling. My guide estimated that this was about half the cave's current bat numbers, though not necessarily an indication of the future population. The gestation period of these tiny mammals ranges from three to five months, and the females can get pregnant twice a year.

As we watched, some of the bats, a red-brown color, with snub-nosed flat faces and pointed ears, scudded nervously along the ceiling and walls. A large group moved off and began to fly up and down the cave's 12-foot-wide corridor. The force of their wings fanning the air turned the cave into a wind tunnel. My companion pulled me against a wall to give them room to pass, and just then a bat bumped my leg. "They usually don't bite humans," he said, "unless you try to handle them." We turned off our lights and the sound of rushing wind immediately began to subside.

My ultimate objective in the southern Oriental was a terrifyingly deep hole in the ground known as Sótano de las Golondrinas, the Pit of the Swallows—actually a misnomer, since the birds that inhabit the pit are swifts and parakeets. Only a few skilled cavers, using nylon ropes, have ever descended into this *sótano*. Measuring the depth from the lowest point on the rim to the point directly below it on the bottom, they arrived at a figure of 1,091 feet. In fact, at one point the floor of the shaft is 1,306 feet deep, and passages extend below that to a depth of more than 1,700 feet. "Golondrinas is so big it's hard to appreciate," Dwight Deal told me. "You have to drop a rock and watch it start to

The plant known in Mexico as mala mujer—bad woman—spreads broad leaves to a shaft of sunlight in its forest habitat. Deceptively harmless in appearance, mala mujer's leaves, stalks and fruit contain a corrosive fluid that, on contact with human skin, causes a sting as virulent as a wasp's and intense pain for several hours.

wobble and float before you realize the scale. Or you lean over the rim and see what looks like a fly coming up and then it turns out to be a green parakeet.''

Deal, Ron Ralph and I set out for Golondrinas on a warm morning in early January. Our starting point was Ciudad de Valles, 100 miles below the Tropic of Cancer, and as we hiked southwest through the mountains I became aware of the sharp differences between this part of the Oriental range and its northern reaches. Now we were in a rain forest, lush and lively and thick with foliage. Yet the soil that spawns this abundant verdure is curiously shallow; it barely covers the limestone beneath. The ground is more rock than dirt—trees send their roots down through cracks in the limestone—and streams are rare even though rainfall is heavy. In fact, all the classic conditions of a well-developed karst landscape are present, including the great vertical shafts of the *sótanos.*

To get to Golondrinas we had to hike over two ridges and partway up a third, traveling a rocky trail that natives of the roadless region had cut through the forest. For the first few hours the trail slanted sharply upward. We labored along under our packs, drinking in the sensory delights of the jungle: bright orange and blue butterflies; olive-colored *chachalacas,* birds about the size of bantam chickens, cackling to match their names; lazy-leafed banana trees; an unidentifiable swarm of green-leafed shrubs crowding the trailside. It was an inhabited jungle, to be sure. People and burros moved along the trail, packing coffee beans to the village of Aquismón where the paved road from Ciudad de Valles ends and returning with water and supplies. We passed tin-roofed huts walled with untrimmed branches. A farmer's fat turkey sat in mid-trail and refused to budge. Three boys came by with burlap bags full of wood. *"Buenos días,"* they said cheerfully.

Deal pointed out a trickle of water emerging from between two boulders. "Springs crop up along the faults in uplifted limestone," he explained. "Most every village is built near such a spring; otherwise the water problem is pretty rough." He leaned down and plucked a small plant from the ground. Its root spread almost horizontally through perhaps an inch of earth. "See how shallow the soil is? This whole tropical garden is growing on about that much soil."

A black-and-white-striped millipede inched across the trail. Farther along a battalion of harvester ants marched solemnly by in parade formation, some of them carrying tiny triangular patches of green leaves that fluttered like military flags. A small, raucous band of bright-green parrots, each about a foot long, flew past. At least, I thought they were parrots, until my friends informed me that the birds were parakeets, possibly the ones that lived in our *sótano*.

We camped that night in a thatch-roofed, open-sided shelter at the intersection of two trails, awakening to a thick morning mist that soon cleared to reveal an astonishing spectacle. Parakeets were soaring by us in groups of two, three and four, their brilliant-green bodies lustrous in the sunlight. All around them, flying at high speed, were great swarms of black swifts. The residents of Sótano de las Golondrinas were off in search of their daily bread. I could see now why these white-throated swifts might have been mistaken for swallows. Though their wings are more scythelike, their size—no more than six inches long—and their markings are similar to those of some swallows, with touches of white at the throat, breast and on the rump.

We hoisted our backpacks and started up the trail, passing an occasional hut with a yard full of dark-red coffee berries drying in the sun. Here and there the undergrowth had been cleared, exposing jagged, pitted pinnacles of limestone. A strong baritone voice was singing a love song somewhere beyond the trailside shrubs. Two women passed, carrying pails of water on their heads.

I expressed my surprise at all the evidences we were seeing of human habitation. "Mexicans and Americans differ in their concepts of wilderness," Deal explained to me. "Mexicans can't afford to let any resources go untouched, even in wilderness areas like this one. All the land we're passing through is privately owned, with individual plots of up to ten acres.

"Remember," he went on, "not all wilderness is above ground. Underground areas can be considered true wilderness areas even if the surface land is put to economic use. Every underground resource in Mexico, caves included, is government owned. That's why we had to get permission to go into Gruta del Palmito, and we're also going to need it to visit Golondrinas."

At midday we arrived at the village where we were to secure the permission from the local *juez*, or judge, only to learn from his wife that he was in another village farther along our route. But we tarried awhile. Children surrounded us, the bravest reaching out to touch our backpacks. "*Vengan, gringos aqui*," they called to their friends, summoning them to see the *norteamericanos*.

The two dozen structures that constituted the village were snuggled

A flight of green parakeets (above) wings past a limestone wall inside the awesome pit called Sótano de las Golondrinas (right), where they roost each night on ledges and in crevices. The walls of the pit—which also houses huge flocks of swifts—plunge more than a quarter of a mile from the tree-fringed rim to the bottom.

serenely if somewhat precipitously near the top of a ridge along one of the spring-producing faults. We sat down in the placid square and drank lukewarm soft drinks. A venerable Huastec Indian, barefoot and wearing a one-piece white garment, nodded gravely at us. Well on in years, he bore the strong features that distinguish his people. "Interesting thing about the Huastecs," Ralph said. "They are Catholics now, but they retain their belief in a deity known as Earth Owner, and think that he lives in a cave."

Late that afternoon, having found the judge and received his written approval for our venture, we started up the side of our third and last ridge—the one in which Golondrinas lies. In the hazy distance we could see the flat, green plain spreading eastward to the Gulf of Mexico. Eager to reach the *sótano* before the sun went down, we stepped up our pace and virtually galloped the last half mile. Suddenly a huge black cloud blocked out the sun—the swifts, thousands of them, were swirling around in a vast circle. We were hell-bent now, stumbling through the underbrush looking for shortcuts to the pit, knowing that the swifts were circling it prior to roosting for the night. I became conscious of a loud, continuous whooshing sound, the noise of thousands of pairs of wings beating the air.

At last we came out of a forest of sweet gum and oak, and there, only a few yards ahead of us down a 10° slope, was the lip of the pit itself. Swifts were dive bombing into it by the hundreds, hurtling past us with such speed that they were little more than black blurs. The entire scene was one huge sensory explosion: the great clouds of birds, the rush of air as they roared into the pit, the jungle around its edges and the pit itself—dark and seemingly fathomless. We dropped to our knees and crawled cautiously to the overhanging edge. The bordering rock was fissured and pitted with crevices, so it was possible to wedge a foot or a knee and feel reasonably, though by no means totally, secure. I felt as if I were at the edge of a sloping roof on the Empire State Building.

As the swifts continued to circle in huge swarms, then swoop, I tried to make out the bottom of the pit. "What's on the floor?" I asked. "Guano," Ralph said.

During our frantic scramble to get to the pit, we had all picked up rocks. Now Ralph pulled out a stop watch and Deal dropped the first rock. It fell straight down, then appeared to wobble and drift before it disappeared from sight. Ralph pressed the watch button when we heard a resonant *thunk*. "Ten-point-three seconds," he said. We tried again: 10.5. And again: 10.8. A flat rock went down in 12.7 seconds. I was getting a lesson in basic physics: different shapes of rock encounter variations in air resistance, with the result that they differ in the velocity at which they fall.

The storm of swifts was finally beginning to abate, and now we noticed the parakeets, chattering noisily. They had simply been waiting their turn. Little groups of them—from three to 10—appeared out of the trees and began making long, lazy loops around the top of the pit. They spiraled downward in easy stages, their shiny, almost fluorescent green plumage growing dimmer and dimmer until they were specks in the dark tube. Half a dozen groups were in the air at any one time; when they had all entered the pit, half a dozen more showed up. The parakeets were more sedate than the swifts. It was as if the swifts were the kids, the parakeets were the teachers and the end-of-recess bell had just rung, summoning all of them back into the schoolhouse.

How many birds live in this pit? How many leaves has the forest? The scene was mesmerizing, a glimpse of nature at its wildest and most beautiful. "I'd kind of like to go down there," Ron said quietly. Both he and Deal had the know-how to make the 1,100-foot free fall, but they had not brought the equipment. A free fall is a descent by rope in which the rope hangs completely free of the walls of the hole, and the caver dangles like a spider on a thread. Climbing in and out of a pit such as Golondrinas requires a tremendous amount of rope rigged through a metal brake rack to control speed, a sling harness and movable foot loops for the arduous climb up and out.

Golondrinas is not a straight, cylindrical shaft, as it appears from the rim, but bells out as it descends. At the top, its dimensions are about 160 feet by 205 feet, at the bottom, 440 feet by 1,000 feet—a floor area about six acres in size. "The first caver who got to the bottom in 1967 was amazed at how big it was," Deal said. "He wandered around for a while and then discovered he had lost sight of the end of his climbing rope. He finally got back to it after finding his own footprints and retracing them."

Ralph mentioned an even more unnerving experience he himself had undergone at another sótano. Together with several other cavers, he had obtained what the group thought were all the necessary permissions from local officials. But because of a misunderstanding caused by some confusing instructions in Spanish, they had inadvertently failed to contact one minor functionary. Angry that his permission had not been sought, he ordered the climbing rope pulled up while Ralph and his companion were on the bottom. They remained there for several hours before another official intervened and the rope was redropped. "When that rope hit the ground we were on it," Ralph recalled. "We kept bumping into each other on the way and it only took us a half hour to get up." A normal, unhurried ascent, he estimated, would have taken a couple of hours.

I asked Deal to tell me just how an outsize pit like Golondrinas came to be. He explained that it originated when ground water seeped downward at the intersection of a major fault and an exceptionally well-developed zone of vertical fractures in the rock. The limestone was gradually dissolved and small openings in it were enlarged, forming a big, water-filled underground chamber. The water in this ever-growing chamber continued to percolate downward along the fissures, dissolving the limestone as it went. The amount of limestone removed by solution to form the main shaft of Golondrinas, Deal estimated, was an almost incredible 200 million cubic feet—five times the volume of Gruta del Palmito.

Golondrinas probably became an open pit after the water drained and the original chamber ceiling collapsed and blocks of its walls fell in, filling the bottom with hundreds of feet of breakdown. Today relatively little surface water enters the pit, though a small waterfall issues from one side of it after heavy rains. But, cavers report, the blocks on the pit floor appear to be dissolving. "It seems that this pit and others in the area are still growing deeper," Deal said. "The next generation of cavers may have to bring even longer ropes."

As we talked, the bird show ended, reminding us abruptly that it was nearly dark. We pitched our tents in a grassy clearing about 100 yards from the pit. "Watch out for the *mala mujer;* it's all over," Ralph said as we gathered wood. *Mala mujer* (in English, bad woman) is probably the most-avoided plant in Mexico, a narrow-trunked, 10-foot shrub with spiny hairs on its leaves and stalks that cause a stinging rash fiercely painful to the skin.

The next morning we awoke just after sunrise to a tornado of swifts zooming 30 feet above our tents. We dressed and hurried to the edge of the pit. The swifts were exploding out of the shaft like rocks from an erupting volcano. Peering over the lip, we could hear the wind from their wings echoing in the hole. The birds were shooting straight up and out, then swarming together and taking off eastward, whizzing close over the tops of the trees.

We were so absorbed in the spectacle that at first we failed to notice a teen-age boy standing on a nearby boulder. He was holding a long, flat stick and swatting at the swifts as they emerged; the stick made a sharp, whipping sound as he swung it, leaning precariously over the pit's edge. After a few minutes he climbed down to where we were. In one hand he held a single swift—the morning's harvest. He told us that he came here every morning and that he killed two or three birds a day on the average. I asked if anyone had ever fallen in; he said he had heard that another boy had fallen, 20 years ago.

"Why do you kill the birds?" Deal asked.

"To eat. There is no other reason," he replied.

Now the parakeets were beginning to glide gracefully out of the pit. They were leisurely; their long, spiraling flight pattern seemed much less compulsive than that of the swifts. They moved slowly into the day, pausing on the limb of a cliffside shrub to screak among themselves before flying off lazily. The youthful bird hunter showed no interest in them; they were clever enough to elude his stick.

More parakeets kept coming out for 20 or 30 minutes before the place fell quiet again. A tiny hummingbird hovered a few feet out over the pit. I wondered if it realized where it was. Then, with a sudden explosion, another flock of swifts shot out of the pit. Late sleepers? The clean-up detail? They had waited for the parakeets to complete their exodus before they took off.

We squirmed along the sloping rock for a final look into the *sótano*. It was silent, a huge dark city now emptied of its commuting citizens. Morning sunlight moved slowly down the western wall. I wondered what the first Indian to come across this pit had thought about it. Maybe he thought it was Earth Owner's house. Maybe it is.

NATURE WALK / In Cuatro Ciénegas Basin

Opening my eyes at sunrise, I was both dazzled and confused by a unique expanse of desert and all it held. Fortunately, for a guide I had Tom Wendt, a bearded graduate student in botany at the University of Texas and an experienced desert explorer. Wendt, photographer Dan Budnik and I had spent the night bedded down among gypsum flats and dunes on the floor of a small basin called Cuatro Ciénegas, or four marshes, in the Chihuahuan Desert some 160 miles south-southwest of Big Bend National Park.

On the way here, Tom had told us that the basin, roughly 40 miles square, has no drainage outlet and is thus an example—though atypical —of the land form called a bolson (pages 136-147), which is common in the northern Sierra Madre. This particular basin is bisected by the Sierra de San Marcos, a range near the northern end of the Sierra Madre Oriental. We were in the western half of the basin. From my sleeping bag I could look in all directions to distant cordilleras: nearest was the San Marcos, a long, inclined plane backlit by the rising sun.

Beyond my line of vision but very much in my thoughts were the marshes that lay between us and the mountains, receiving their water neither from mountain streams nor direct rainfall. The principal source of water for the marshes—and the source, too, of the gypsum that covers so much of the basin—is a series of thermal springs that rise near the protruding tip of the San Marcos mountains. These springs, aided by an intricate system of subterranean passageways that funnel ground water from beneath the mountains, nourish the special environment of Cuatro Ciénegas. In this meeting place of desiccating desert and oozing wetland exists an astonishing mixture of animal and plant species found nowhere else.

During the November day now dawning we planned to hike from our camp on the basin floor, around the marshes to a small canyon in the Sierra de San Marcos—six miles, perhaps, as the crow flies, considerably farther as we wandered through a variety of habitats. But before we even broke camp, we were rewarded by the sight of a rare yellow flower poking its head above the rim of a neighboring gypsum dune. Called scientifically *Dyssodia gypsophilia,* it grows only here. It is related to dogweed but has no common name. We dubbed it gypsum dogweed.

Inside the gypsum dogweed lurked a crab spider, a far-ranging, adaptable arachnid. Lying in wait for the pollinating insects they prey on, some crab-spider species can assume the exact hue of a variety of white and yellow flowers. Another ubiquitous desert dweller near our camp was the red-fruited tasajillo,

CRAB SPIDER UPON A DYSSODIA

DESERT CHRISTMAS-CACTUS FRUITS

or desert Christmas cactus. Beware of this plant. Its spines produce a nasty, festering wound. A second common plant growing close by, sprouting among low-lying *Ericameria,* was ocotillo, a long spiny shrub, leafless at the beginning of the dry season. But although ocotillo occurs in other places in the desert, it is only in the Cuatro Ciénegas region that this species appears in intimate association with gypsum.

OCOTILLO AND ERICAMERIA ON GYPSUM FLATS

In the basin of Cuatro Ciénegas the gypsum assumes two guises. It lies in compacted gray flats where weathering of the surface has produced a semistable crust, allowing plants and shrubs to take hold. Quite different are the living, moving, dazzling white gypsum dunes that rise 20 to 30 feet above the desert floor. Both forms originate in shallow lakes—such as Laguna Grande about a mile and a half east of our campground—which are part of the system of marshes fed by the warm springs. The spring waters are rich in gypsum and other dissolved minerals. As the water evaporates and the lakes shrink in the dry season, gypsum crystallizes at the margins. The prevailing east wind whips the dry crystals and flakes into billowing dunes, which are slowly and constantly on the move. The gray flats are remnants of dunes long passed.

When we arrived the previous evening, the pristine curves of the dunes had beckoned to us across the flats. Now, come morning, we examined one of the dunes more closely. We looked first at its front wall, arrested momentarily on this windless day in the act of overrunning an area of stabilized gypsum. The ground-hugging plants and grasses at the base of the dune were doomed. Others, like the yucca called Spanish dagger with its spiky green top and shaggy trunk already partly engulfed, might be able to grow fast enough to keep their heads above sand. The mesquite and saltbush higher up had been able to do so.

Animal life was harder to find,

MESQUITE, YUCCA AND SALTBUSH ATOP A GYPSUM DUNE

BLISTER BEETLE ON A MOONPOD STEM

WOLF SPIDER

particularly by day. In the desert the sun is more enemy than friend. Still, its warm hand on our backs was welcome after the chill desert night.

Dan spotted a blister beetle clinging to a moonpod bush. Blister beetles—there are hundreds of species throughout the American Southwest and Mexico—are so called because they produce a toxin that causes a burning rash on contact with human skin. As for the moonpod bush, whose name may derive from its round, greenish-yellow fruit, it is a rare shrub and its presence was one of the treats of our walk in Cuatro Ciénegas. Large portions of the moonpod bush routinely die during drought, but a few green twigs nurture the spark of life.

Two Tiny Predators

We had to dig for two other discoveries. We found a wolf spider some six inches down by opening up its burrow, the mouth of which was a small hole with a delicate half-inch-high lip of gypsum crystals raised around it. Wolf spiders are aggressive hunters, and many species

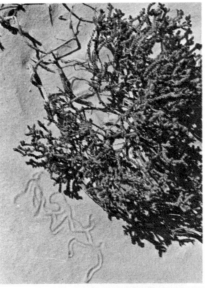

MACHAERANTHERA AND ANTLION TRACK

ANTLION AMID GYPSUM CRYSTALS

of this family do not spin webs for catching prey. But they do use silk for other purposes—in this case to cement the crystals around the hole and line their burrows. Our specimen, a nocturnal hunter, at first seemed stunned by the light, but soon scurried off under a saltbush.

Even more intriguing than the spider's hole was the odd-looking track we found beside a ropelike plant, endemic to Cuatro Ciénegas, that Tom told us had no popular name but was identified scientifically as *Machaeranthera restiformis*. This strange tracery on the ground grew longer as we watched. The hidden artist, which we dug up a few moments later, turned out to be the larval form of an antlion. Ordinarily antlion larvae dig pits in the sand and wait at the bottom for prey to fall in. This antlion, moving just beneath the surface, may have been looking for a site to dig its pit. While doing so, it left an aimless spoor in the sand, thus living up to its other common name, doodlebug.

After breakfast, around nine, we

GYPSUM CONGEALED AROUND MESQUITE

started hiking eastward toward the mountains over the crest of the dunes. The high wispy clouds visible at dawn had evaporated and the sky radiated an intense, almost searing blue. Coming down off the back of the dunes we found ourselves standing in an area studded with haystack-like mounds, some of them about 18 feet high. Tom explained how they had formed: as the wind licked at the back of the dunes, pushing the loose sand forward, the extensive root systems of the bushes growing on them, mostly mesquite, held onto some of the gypsum.

Not only do the roots form a skeletal structure but, by releasing chemical substances, they seem actually to cement the gypsum crystals into a coherent mass. As the loose material gradually blows past, the mounds remain.

It appears, however, that the mesquite tree is capable of only a temporary holding action. In spite of the roots, the mounds gradually decay, for the nutrients become ex-hausted and eventually the mesquite dies. The mound then dries out and crumbles away, its remains slowly spreading throughout the area.

Another casualty of the shifting dunes is the Spanish dagger. As we had seen at the front of the dune we examined, this handsome member of the yucca family sometimes grows a long trunk to keep its head above the top of the sand. When the sand blows away, however, the trunk collapses. But the plant often continues to live. We saw several thriving yuccas growing atop old, gnarled, doubled-over trunks.

On the other hand, a plant like the little red-stemmed gypsum spurge cannot even gain a foothold on the high dunes. Instead, it moves in as the dunes pass, colonizing the flats in low-growing tangles about two feet across.

Finding the Source of the Dunes

Beyond the back of the dunes we crossed a mile or two of largely barren salt flats. Only months ago the *laguna* flooded this plain and even now

SELENITE CRYSTALS

the water table lay just under the surface. But the crumbly residue of gypsum and other minerals left by the retreating lake was too alkaline to permit germination of plant life.

Predominant among the minerals were patches of selenite, the crystalline form of gypsum. These little deposits, about the size of grains of rice, were the basic building blocks of the mighty dunes. Tumbled by the wind, they would be abraded down to particles the size of granulated sugar; and at the same time they would be gathered together until they formed a shifting mass.

After walking for about half an

COLLAPSED YUCCA PLANTS

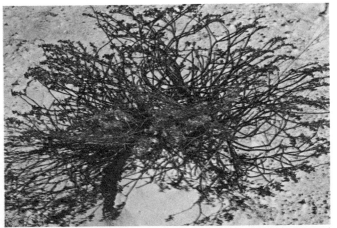

GYPSUM SPURGE

hour we came to the fringes of Laguna Grande. It had first appeared as a glassy ribbon shimmering like a mirage on the basin floor.

On a gypsum mound we came upon a robber fly feeding on a butterfly. This savage insect descends like a hawk, seizing its prey—other flies, bees and wasps—from behind. Sinking its stout beak into its victim the robber fly paralyzes it with venom and then sucks out the fluids.

Long before we reached the lake itself, the ground grew damp. Soon we were splashing through very shallow puddles. We took off our boots and waded the last few hundred yards to the edge of the open lake. On the way we came upon the first large and spectacular flowers we had seen in Cuatro Ciénegas. This one was a beauty. A marsh pink, Tom called it, about the size of a 50-cent piece and common to coastal wetlands throughout the American South and into the West Indies. In central and northern Mexico, however, it grows only in widely separated inland marshy areas.

A Rare Turtle

We waded into the water, which seemed cool after our hot walk. Mud oozed up between our toes. All at once we spotted a turtle lying on the lake bottom in a couple of feet of water. It made no effort to escape as I waded toward it—strange behavior for an aquatic turtle, usually an agile swimmer. And when I picked it up it simply pulled in its legs, head and tail and closed shop by folding its bottom shell up tight against its carapace. It was a box turtle, and a

ROBBER FLY WITH PREY

MARSH PINK IN FLOWER

LAGUNA GRANDE

BOX TURTLE UNDERWATER

species of the normally land-bound genus *Terrapene*, the star inhabitants of Cuatro Ciénegas.

These small reptiles, known locally as black turtles, grow up to nine inches long, and some years ago their presence triggered a detailed scientific study of Cuatro Ciénegas. Biologically speaking, the basin was not discovered until 1939, when an adventurous American naturalist, E. G. Marsh Jr., began a collection of plants and animals here. The Second World War prevented Marsh's material from receiving the attention it deserved, but from the mid-'40s on, as Marsh's specimens were examined and classified, the list of species unique to Cuatro Ciénegas grew.

The first indication of the significance of the box turtle came in 1958, when John M. Legler and W. L. Minckley—then both graduate students majoring in zoology at the University of Kansas—studied the specimens and discovered traces of algae on the shells. Algae indicated an aquatic habitat. But box turtles of this genus, they both knew, were terrestrial animals. So they rushed down to Cuatro Ciénegas to see for themselves. Sure enough, this box turtle was a swimmer.

Since then, Minckley and his associates have been in the forefront of investigations that have revealed Cuatro Ciénegas as a fascinating biological island where, among other things, the world's only aquatic *Terrapene* is known to exist.

How this anomaly came to be is a matter of some evolutionary disagreement. It was long thought to have evolved from a terrestrial ancestor, adopting aquatic habits in the wet refuge at Cuatro Ciénegas when the surrounding environment became too dry. Current scientific thinking, however, suggests this species of *Terrapene* may be a primitive form that has been aquatic throughout its long evolutionary life in this locale, where conditions on the basin floor have remained relatively stable despite climatic changes. If so, this particular turtle qualifies as a relict that has maintained its original form while other similar species have evolved quite differently. In any case, our aquatic box turtle, like all other turtles, lays its eggs on land and, like all reptiles, breathes air.

MILKWORT BLOSSOMS

We saw several more turtles before we rounded the northern end of the laguna and reached a narrow watercourse. This tributary, according to our map, would be the Río Churince, which we planned to follow to a series of springs called Posos Bonitos, the river's source. Some river! One hundred yards upstream it was narrow enough to jump across. Yet on closer examina-

SEDGES AND GRASSES BESIDE RÍO CHURINCE

tion, it seemed to carry an impressive amount of water. As it turned out, the Churince was nearly as deep as it was wide, and the banks were sharply undercut—as much as five feet in places. A foot below the surface the river was really twice as wide as it appeared.

I wondered how this had come about, since the current, flowing at about the pace of a slow walk, was hardly sufficient to gouge out the banks. Tom explained that the overhang was not the result of erosion, but rather a combination of plant and mineral growth. Minerals from the rich spring water crystallized like rock candy on the sedges and grasses along the banks. In time, rotted plant material accumulated amid the crystal deposits, and as new plants rooted, the banks grew together. The marsh through which the Río Churince meandered was riddled with streams that had roofed themselves over completely.

There were other surprises in the marsh if one looked closely—for instance, a little plant with a spiky bloom. Tom pointed it out as a succulent polygala, or milkwort. It was the only such milkwort he knew of —and he should know because desert milkworts were the subject of his doctoral thesis. This polygala, as far as anyone is aware, grows only at Cuatro Ciénegas and at similar moist meadows to the south. Close to it we found another plant blooming, a thistle of a type common throughout the American Southwest.

Here and there the vegetation was interrupted by small stagnant pud-

THISTLE HEADS

SALT POOL STAINED BY BACTERIA

ALLIGATOR LIZARD

dles with crusted margins. The puddles were mahogany in color, the shade deepening with the concentration of the brew. I had seen oceanside salt flats exhibiting a similarly ruddy color, produced by salt-loving bacteria. The same biological factor was at work here.

An Unexpected Lizard

At the edge of one of these miniature clearings Dan spotted a well-camouflaged, six-inch-long brown lizard, its ribs flecked with white. He and Tom agreed that it was a species of alligator lizard. Although they are very fast when striking prey —beetles and small insects—they are relatively slow moving otherwise, and we were able to follow its deliberate steps while Dan clicked away. We did not want to handle it, for when caught by the tail, an alligator lizard is likely to shuck that appendage while wriggling free.

Later, when we showed Dan's pictures to a herpetologist, he easily identified the lizard as *Gerrhonotus liocephalus*. That meant we had scored a genuine scoop. The lizard lives throughout much of the Chihuahuan Desert and has even been collected before in the region of Cuatro Ciénegas, but always at higher altitudes. It is an upland lizard, at home in damp forests, and this was the first time our consultant had heard of one being found on a basin floor. The story of how it got there was another matter. Perhaps, like the turtle, it was a relict that had managed to survive.

By noon we were close to the source of the Río Churince. In a few

VEJOVIS COAHUILAE SCORPION

MATING DAMSELFLIES

on species. It turned out that we had a good find, though not quite an endemic: this fellow, delicate as glass, belligerent as a bull, turned out to be *Vejovis coahuilae,* found only here and in Pecos County, Texas —some 260 miles away.

Ahead of us a heron flew up—a great blue, judging from its size. We made our approach to the *poso* stealthily, hoping to see more water birds. In this we were disappointed, yet the pool was vibrant with life. The buzz of insects filled the air. We stopped to watch a pair of damselflies perform their mating ritual on a rapier blade of a bulrush. The iridescent blue male had seized the female by the neck with claspers at the extreme end of his elongated abdomen. Momentarily the female would curve her own abdomen under her partner to touch his sperm duct, completing both the mating act and a perfect geometric figure.

At last we came to the main pool. It was about 30 yards in diameter and 10 to 15 feet deep at the center, with abrupt banks. And it demanded to be dived into. We had brought a pair of underwater goggles, which we took turns using. What enchantment! It was like swimming in an aquarium. In the center of the pool, at the bottom, I could actually see water pulsing up through the sediments from underground springs.

An Outpost of Evolution

Hundreds of stubby black-spotted fish, about a half foot long, glided about, untroubled by our presence. They belonged to the cichlid family, perchlike fresh-water fish common

hours we had walked from Laguna Grande—which I had come to regard as the Mediterranean of this water system—up the Churince to Posos Bonitos, the enchanting pools from which it rises. I thought of the Nile, and of the years spent discovering its source. Europe, Africa and Cuatro Ciénegas: a farfetched analogy? Perhaps. But the similarity between this oasis and the Mediterranean—both surrounded by mountains and desert—lingered in my mind.

I was still lost in this reverie when Dan turned up a scorpion under some matted weeds. I wondered immediately whether it was one of Cuatro Ciénegas' 11 endemic scorpi-

to Africa and Asia, and occurring in tropical and subtropical waters both there and, less frequently, in the Americas. To my eye they all looked alike, but actually they represented four of the species endemic to Cuatro Ciénegas. Like the box turtles, they were particularly revealing illustrations of the workings of evolution. Taxonomists have discovered that one of these fish has thick, heavy teeth and strong jaw muscles to crush snails. Another, identical externally, has fine teeth and lacks powerful crushing jaws; it feeds on soft bottom debris. Two additional species have more streamlined bodies as well as strong jaws; they prey on other fish.

Isolated for tens of thousands of years, the ancestral cichlid had evolved into four species, each with a different feeding apparatus. Had the waters of the Cuatro Ciénegas basin been filled with more efficient competitors, such diversification might not have occurred.

We were greatly tempted to linger

BULRUSHES AND CATTAILS AT POSOS BONITOS

CICHLIDS NEAR THE POND BOTTOM

GRUSONIA AND LECHUGUILLA ON THE BAJADA

at the *poso,* but after eating lunch we topped off our canteens—despite its high mineral content this water has no salty taste—and set off toward the San Marcos. The change was as abrupt as if we had set sail from a lush island into a hostile sea. Our ocean was the bajada, the alluvial slope that rises up the front wall of the San Marcos. Its surface is a composite of boulders, gravel and sand. The finer particles have been washed farther away from the mountains, so that the way became increasingly rough.

We had some three miles of bajada to cross to reach the mouth of the canyon that we had chosen as our destination. Cicadas chirruped loudly from the brush; a covey of scaled quail, so named for the look of their plumage, flew up ahead of us. But that was all the animal life we came across. The vegetation was anything but scarce.

Creosote bush is so abundant that Mexicans call it *gobernadora,* or governor, because of its dominance. The English name derives from the heavy, resinous odor of the foliage similar to that of the sticky oils used to preserve wood. After a rainstorm, Tom told us, the air is redolent with it. He liked it, he said. I would as soon sniff a railroad tie.

Two particular plants imprinted themselves indelibly on our minds. The first was *Grusonia,* a low cactus that grows in thick patches and occurs only in Cuatro Ciénegas and westward for about 100 miles. Its pulpy segmented body glistens with shiny off-white needles. Everything

LECHUGUILLA FRUIT

LECHUGUILLA FLOWERS

about *Grusonia* says look but keep your distance.

Even more dangerous is lechuguilla, like maguey a member of the large agave family. At first glance a stand of lechuguilla seems to admit passage. But its openings lure the hiker into ever narrower twisting corridors that close in and become traps.

A Thorny Passage

Lechuguilla's weaponry of spines is borne on stiff leathery leaves that grow from a central core, like lettuce. In fact, lechuguilla means little lettuce in Spanish, perhaps because it was an extremely important food for the early Indians who ate the heart of the plant. Mature plants are typically about a foot high and the margins of the leaves are lined with curved spines. But it is the longer, stouter spines at the ends of the leaves that do the real damage. They readily puncture trousers and even leather, and leave nasty wounds.

Like other agaves, each lechuguilla rosette blooms only once in its lifetime. At the age of between 10 and 25 years—depending on how much moisture the growing plant has received—lechuguilla sends up one spike studded with flowers that vary between shades of red, green and yellow. As these develop into little green fruit, the main rosette dies but a dozen or so shoots spring up around its base. Seeds reside inside the fruit, and if an extended drought kills the shoots, the seeds eventually germinate anyway.

Unlike *Grusonia*, which has no useful purpose, lechuguilla is still harvested, albeit for new purposes.

Its root makes the basis of a good shampoo and fibre from its leaves can be made into twine. For us, however, it proved merely an obstacle to be gotten around.

As we drew closer to the mountain the bajada became steeper. Erosion had eaten deeply into the slope, and we found ourselves climbing up a dry wash with high banks —the entrance to our canyon. Walking in the wash proved easier than on the open flat, however, since here the prickly vegetation had been swept away by flash floods.

At the entrance to the canyon itself we came upon a sotol growing in a cleft in the rock. Wind, funneling down the arroyo, had whipped its leaves about until they had actually worn a circular pattern into the limestone, a graphic example of the toughness of the plants that

SOTOL ON SCOURED ROCK

survive in such a harsh country.

Inside the narrow canyon, we stepped into shadow and at once were bathed in new sensations. Though there were no seeps or damp spots, on every hand were signs of water. The canyon we had selected is one of the major drainages of the northwest side of the Sierra de San Marcos, and it contains an arroyo that funnels rain water down the mountainside and onto the bajada. Furthermore, the shaded walls keep water from evaporating as rapidly as it does elsewhere. Wasps, bees, flies and beetles animated the air. Birds called, and there were a few stunted, leafy trees and bushes: acacias, hackberries, desert willows, desert ashes and some small oaks.

At first view the canyon seemed to be a dead end. But as we clam-

INSIDE THE CANYON

bered up the rocks toward a sun-washed scarp, we found that what appeared to be the head of the canyon was merely a right-angle turn. We were in a zigzag fissure that ran deep into the heart of the range between sheer cliffs.

As we came around the turn, all sight of the basin vanished. We were confined, pressed in upon, a strange feeling after the openness of the land behind. It made one dizzy to look up at rocks stacked in impossible piles, ready at the slightest provocation, it seemed, to come crashing down. Some of those that already had fallen were the size of frame houses. The thought of being caught here in a flood was frightening. This was a grinding machine, this canyon and hundreds like it. As these huge boulders were undercut and pushed by flash floods roaring over the canyon floor, they shifted and rolled, grinding up the material that spewed out onto the bajada.

Now only a brisk breeze came down the canyon. Its welcome coolness reminded us that we had to climb back down and recross the bajada before dark. There would be some light from a three-quarters moon, but we did not want to have to pick our way through the *Gruso-nia* and lechuguilla with flashlights.

We came out of the canyon to the head of the bajada just as the sun was setting. At my shoulder, a blind prickly-pear cactus thrust its way out of the rock wall. The basin lay before us, the dunes we had slept on the night before looking like water in the waning light.

BLIND PRICKLY PEAR GROWING FROM CANYON CREVICE

3/ Where the Birds Are

I am forced to abstain from enumerating every kind of bird,
for there was everything from the
Royal Eagle down to tiny birds of many-coloured plumage.

BERNAL DÍAZ DEL CASTILLO/ *THE DISCOVERY AND CONQUEST OF MEXICO 1517-1521*

At a village called Gómez Farías the pavement ended. The drive on a brand-new road off the Pan American Highway had been only a short one, but in the village square the cogs of time seemed to have slipped a century or two. I parked in somebody's front yard under mango trees, then transferred my duffel to the back of a waiting truck fitted with facing wooden benches. Overhead a welded iron frame carried a canvas cover, furled now since no rain threatened. All corners and hard surfaces in the truck were padded, a precaution I appreciated as soon as the vehicle lurched out of town and began its whining, grinding, bumping ascent of an ancient logging road. I held tight, but when I arrived at Rancho del Cielo nearly two hours later, I had acquired some bruises.

Sky Ranch, to give the place its English name, nestles at 3,750 feet on the side of a block of the Sierra Madre Oriental called the Sierra de Guatemala. Since 1964 it has served Texas Southmost College, a junior college headquartered in Brownsville, as a research station for the study of the area's flora and fauna. A richer location would be hard to find. The lush valley below is one of the northernmost tropical environments in North America. And surrounding the rancho is a cloud forest, where a unique mingling of tropical and temperate plants supports an amazing array of bird life.

On the late December afternoon when I arrived, a primeval dankness permeated the cloud forest, and a chill was in the air. In the cabin assigned to me, the wood fire crackling in the Franklin stove was welcome. I stood with my back to the warmth while Fred Webster, a retired agricultural statistician and the man who had arranged for my visit, outlined rancho's regimen. Right now, he explained, water was scarce. A gopher had chewed a hole in the line from the main reservoir and before it could be fixed, months of accumulated rain, gathered from cabin eaves, had drained away into the porous limestone substructure of the mountain. A few downpours would alleviate the shortage but until then no showers were allowed. The flush toilets were off bounds, too, so guests would have to use the outhouse—at least during daylight hours. After nightfall the ban on indoor plumbing did not apply. Barbara Warburton, chairman of Texas Southmost's Department of Natural Science and founder and manager of the rancho's research station, did not want anyone meeting a bear or a panther in the dark. Bears and panthers? Yes, Webster told me, I would be surprised at what prowled the compound while I slept. For good measure he mentioned the jaguar, el tigre of the Sierra Madre.

Moments later, as I stowed my gear in a bedroom just big enough for twin double-decked bunks and two chests of drawers, I was brought up short by a rude noise—the blaat from an aerosol-powered foghorn. Dinnertime, Webster said; the same blaat would signal breakfast.

In the fading light I stumbled up a rocky path to the dining hall, whose porch commanded a view of a sloping forest glen. Along the path were cultivated plants indigenous to climates farther north: showy azaleas and dwarf peach and pear trees in bloom. In front of the dining hall was a flat marble tombstone, on which was carved "John William Francis Harrison, Born June 21, 1901, Ontario, Canada—Murdered Rancho del Cielo, Mexico, January 29, 1966." It was Harrison who had planted the flowers and the trees, who had in fact established the rancho and literally given his life for it, as I was to learn.

Six cabins rimmed the compound. Beyond them the forest rose, dark with mystery. But inside, warm and comfortable, we ate dinner by gaslight. The food was basic U.S.A., cooked and served by bright-faced coeds from Texas Southmost, seeming as out of place on this wild Mexican mountain as were the foghorns and hybrid azaleas. The dinner conversation helped orient me to my surroundings. The eastern wall of the Sierra de Guatemala, on which the rancho perches, is so steep, I was told, that one can stand on a prominence outside the station clearing and look down over the treetops at farmers burning cane in fields on the coastal plain, more than 3,000 feet below. Above the rancho, the si-

Under a canopy decked in quetzal feathers, Aztec ruler Moctezuma greets conquistador Cortés in this engraved re-creation of a 1519 scene.

erra climbs steplike in a series of jagged limestone ridges, through an almost perpetual mass of swirling mists to a height of 8,000 feet.

The Mountain, as the people at the rancho call their aerie, lies at the heart of the appealing diversity of habitats that have long made Mexico both home and way station for large numbers of birds. The pre-Columbian peoples worshipped birds, used their feathers for adornment and as articles of trade—and, more mundanely, ate them. The Indians bred, among other species, macaws, parrots and turkeys. The Spanish chronicler Bernal Díaz, who with Cortés and a small band of adventurers entered Mexico City in 1519, was amazed by Moctezuma's aviary, which surpassed any collection of birds known to the Europeans.

In addition to the home-bred birds there were captured ducks and eagles and other bizarre flying creatures that Díaz had never seen before, kept in special boxes where they were meticulously cared for. When Cortés and his men were first presented to Moctezuma, the emperor approached them under "a marvellously rich canopy of green coloured feathers," Díaz reported. The feathers came from the star of the aviary, the quetzal—sometimes called the resplendent trogon. The quetzal's plumes represented valor to the Aztecs, who accordingly embellished their emperors' mantles with them.

Quetzals are the largest of the trogons, a family of tropical woodland birds and the most gorgeously colored of all American feathered creatures. Their great glory is their tail feathers, that hang down more than twice their body length in a brilliant emerald festoon. Although the Aztecs revered the bird, their lavish use of its feathers for ceremonial occasions reduced its numbers. Even after the destruction of the Aztec nation, the quetzal's beautiful plumage continued to be its downfall: during the 19th Century it was exhaustively hunted to supply the millinery trade of the United States and Europe. And although the quetzal was finally placed on the protected list in 1936, it is now rare in Mexico. One reads that the meek shall inherit the earth—and along with the meek, one is tempted to add, the dull and the drab, since so many of the heroic and handsome creatures like the quetzal and the grizzly bear may well be annihilated by man long before inheriting time.

Fortunately, neither the Aztecs nor later hunters managed to significantly reduce much of the rest of Mexico's avian population—either the native species or the awesome flights of transients. Each winter birds from the north congregate in Mexico—sand-hill cranes, geese, ducks, plovers, sandpipers, gulls, terns, flycatchers, swallows, warblers, finches, buntings, sparrows. One champion northern commuter, the American golden plover, leaves Nova Scotia in the fall and apparently flies nonstop over water to Brazil. On its return trip it loops around and flies home mainly over a land route, stopping off in Mexico.

In all there are some 200 species of these visitors from the north —plus a few birds that fly up to Mexico to escape the South American winters. There are also a few Mexican species that fly south to take advantage of the South American summers. And finally, from time to time, a wholly inexplicable visitor will appear—like the Eurasian émigré, the red-throated pipit. Ordinarily, winter migration takes the pipit to Africa, India, Malaysia or Indonesia.

The migrants join a resident population of some 800 species to make a rough total of just over 1,000. The United States and Canada combined have no more than three fourths that number, and very few large exotics. Small wonder, considering the greater variety of environments south of the border. Mexico has two seaboards that surpass in length those of the continental United States. There are deserts in the north and rain forests in the south. There are high mountains of all sorts, separated into a multiplicity of ranges, each with its own environment.

The region around Rancho del Cielo contains most of these habitats compressed into an extraordinarily small area (only the marine environment is missing, and that is compensated for in part by neighboring ponds and swamps). In consequence some 255 species, over a quarter of the count for the entire country, have been seen at one time or another within a few hours' walk of the rancho, making it one of the richest birding stations in North America. And that is primarily why, shortly past Christmas, two Dodge trucks—one of them mine—loaded with expectant bird watchers plus their cameras, tripods, binoculars, telescopes, field guides and rain gear, laboriously ground their way up the Sierra de Guatemala.

The bird watchers, gringos all, were an odd lot. Male and female in equal proportion, they ran the gamut in age from young (from Smith and Princeton) to not-so-young (a gray-haired matron from Texas). Recruited by word of mouth and through ads run in birding publications, they had come to the rancho from all over the United States. There were married couples, singles and married people traveling singly. They had little in common save an insatiable hunger to see birds—to see and to hear them, that is; for let it be known that the term bird watcher is inadequate. To the expert, and these people were almost all experts,

Resting like living leaves on the jungle floor and random shrubs, these butterflies wear protective tints that match the tree bark and foliage of Sierra de Guatemala's deciduous forest. The group of six different species (top) has left its haven among the plants to feed on sodium salts in a mud patch; a pair of copperhead bollas becomes momentarily unwary during mating; but the calico and the malachite are well camouflaged by the vegetation on which they perch.

A CLORINDE ABOVE OTHER SALT FEEDERS

MATING COPPERHEAD BOLLAS

A CALICO AGAINST MOSSY TREE BARK

A MALACHITE ON A GREEN FROND

audible recognition is half the game. A few of this group of birders —the preferred term among aficionados—had been to the rancho before. But most were coming up the mountain for the first time. A group of climbers arriving at Katmandu could hardly have been more alive to the excitement of the moment.

The man who assembled this gathering at the rancho was Webster. A regional editor of the National Audubon Society magazine, *American Birds,* Webster had been visiting the area for 11 years. From his first day, he had become enthralled with the great numbers of species to be seen there, and thought, rightly, that others would be too. But that was to be some years away.

The property then belonged to a Canadian émigré named Frank Harrison—he of the marble tombstone outside the dining hall. Harrison, a self-taught botanist, raised tuberous begonias and amaryllises, which thrived in the damp mountain air. He named his homestead Rancho del Cielo. Aside from an occasional trip down the mountain on foot or mule-back, Harrison lived quietly with his flowers, his cows and his books.

When a handful of ornithologists and botanists and just plain Texans who wanted to get away from it all discovered the charms of the cloud forest, they also discovered Harrison. Glad of the stimulating company, Harrison allowed them to camp on his land, and later permitted several of them to build hunting cabins at the rancho, in return for paying him a modest annual rent. In 1964 after several groups of Texas Southmost students went there on field trips, the college built its own cabin. Barbara Warburton, an early and regular visitor, functioned as director of the field groups. Webster arrived the same year.

All this activity captured the attention of some Mexican itinerants who were scratching out a meager squatter's existence logging and farming on the mountain. Harrison's farm, they reasoned, must contain a gold mine, judging from the buildings that were rising on it. Why should a single gringo have all that while they and their families were so poor? And so in profound ignorance they fell upon Harrison with a hunting knife one day in 1966 while he was doing his morning chores. But instead of dumping the body into a sinkhole, where it would probably never have been found, they lost their nerve and ran. The murderers were quickly apprehended and locked up. Harrison, as it turned out, had deeded his land to a nonprofit Mexican corporation, with the stipulation that the cloud forest be preserved. Texas Southmost has since become the major financial contributor to the rancho, which is administered by the corporation.

Six years after the murder, college students under the firm and imaginative guidance of Mrs. Warburton had transformed the rancho from a few cabins in the woods to an operational biological station with a dining hall, library and dormitories. To help defray expenses, the college had also begun to allow increasing numbers of paying guests to visit the rancho and marvel at its bird life. In 1972, with Webster's enthusiastic help, Mrs. Warburton invited a sizable contingent of birders to participate in the rancho's initial entry into the Kentucky Derby of bird watching, the Audubon Christmas Bird Count. That year marked the 73rd annual running of the Christmas count and the first time any area south of the Río Grande had been permitted to enter.

In this intensely competitive—yet intensely good natured—ornithological competition, each year more than 25,000 birders across the continent fan out in small teams to count birds. Each team is restricted to a search area of 15 miles in diameter and to a single calendar day within about a week on either side of Christmas. Any number of birders can participate. The results are collated and published in the April issue of *American Birds,* enabling the various teams to compare their scores. Straight numerical comparisons, of course, have little meaning to many of the purists; the raw number of, say, sea gulls in Boston or swallows in Capistrano is not what your typical Christmas counter tends to care about. For him the payoff comes in total species recorded —though numbers do have considerable value as preservationist data.

Before 1972, neither Mexico nor any Central American country had been included in the count, for the simple but critical reason that, until then, there had been no heavily illustrated guide to the birds below the border, and hence no sure way to confirm all sightings. But that year two guides came out, each illustrated in color: Irby Davis' *A Field Guide to the Birds of Mexico and Central America* and Ernest P. Edwards' *A Field Guide to the Birds of Mexico.* With these publications in hand and another one promised, Robert Arbib, editor of *American Birds* and arbiter of rules for the Christmas Bird Count, officially included the lands south of the border in the competition. And he tossed in the West Indies for good measure.

That year the rather hastily recruited birders at Rancho del Cielo came in 12th out of 1,013 reporting areas, and only 34 species behind the winning count of 209 recorded by the winners at Cocoa, Florida. Dazzled by this promising start, Texas Southmost decided to make the rancho a permanent entry. In addition, the college instituted a late-spring count. At that season the forest is alive with amorous male birds and the sound of their love songs—seductive, to attract mates, and contentious, to indicate territories and warn other males to stay away.

Thus, bird counting was on its way to becoming an institution at the rancho when I arrived. The big Christmas count was to begin the very next morning, the last day of the year. In addition to the books by Davis and Edwards, I was equipped with a 1973 publication, *A Field Guide to Mexican Birds,* by the dean of bird-guide author-illustrators, Roger Tory Peterson, and co-author Edward L. Chalif.

After supper and my quick, general orientation to the terrain Webster gathered the troops in the cabin that served as a combined library, laboratory and lecture hall. The experienced birders among the visitors numbered 21. Webster, his wife, Marie, and Mrs. Warburton brought the team total to 24 able-bodied counters. Then there were two hopeless novices—me and my 14-year-old daughter, Heather, who had driven across the country with me—and one dog. The latter, as stated on the papers I had needed to get him across the border at Brownsville, Texas, is a shepherd-beagle mix; he answers, when it suits him, to the name Patrick. Webster, after canvassing personal preferences, divided us into six roving platoons—a pitifully inadequate number, he lamented, to cover the area. But the rancho could accommodate no more. Heather and Patrick were to stay around the compound under the wing of a couple called Anderson who knew the rancho and would make good mentors. The cleared land of the compound itself would be a very productive area for counting. Many songbirds like open spaces or forest edges where flowering plants attract insects for the birds to feed on and where grasses provide additional nourishment in the way of seeds.

I was assigned to Mrs. Warburton's party, the rest of which consisted of Jarvis Beverly, a retired petrochemical engineer from Michigan, and two college students, his protégés on this trip. Charles Munn III, a Princeton student, was something of a birding prodigy. Already, at the age of 19, he had been birding on four continents and had a life list of over 700. That is, he had personally seen more than 700 different species of birds—roughly the equivalent of a scratch handicap in golf or a 300-plus batting average. This was his first visit to Mexico, and I would soon learn how well he had done his homework. Mary McKitrick, from Smith, had recently completed a six-month stint at the Manomet Bird Observatory in Massachusetts. Her special interest was bird behavior, and she tactfully dismissed the life-list syndrome as being more closely related to stamp and coin collecting than to serious ornithology. None of which diminished her enthusiasm at being in the proximity of so many new birds.

Our party would roam the farthest. Mrs. Warburton had decided to let us use the rancho's two trucks to cross the Sierra de Guatemala to the vicinity of a small, isolated community, La Joya de Salas. On this dry side of the mountain, the birds differ from those of the cloud forest along the way, so in a single day I would see as much variety both in birds and terrain as the sierra offered. We would be climbing out of the cloud forest up to the moist pine-oak forest at 4,200 feet then on to the top of the mountain and down into a little valley of dry pine-oak forest that lay in the rain shadow on the western slope.

Assignments made, Webster concluded the evening by reviewing the check list of the 255 bird species resident in the region. He had already sent a copy of it to each of us, so that we could bone up on our identifications. Mercifully, as it was growing late, Webster hit only the high spots on the list—the difficult identifications, the rare birds.

The next morning, breakfast was served early enough to get the convoy rolling by sunup. Along the route we dropped three of the other parties, one to be picked up later, the other two to hoof it back to the rancho. By sometime around 10:30, we had joggled and bumped down a winding arroyo and out of the pine-oak forest into sunlight on a flat, winding valley, backed by yet another wrinkle of the Sierra Madre Oriental. La Joya consisted of some two dozen neat stone and adobe houses inside walled gardens. Beyond the settlement, fields of corn stubble and other harvested grains stretched to the visible limit of the valley.

To our left lay a shallow lake and to the right, a marshy pond. Both owed their existence to layers of clay that effectively sealed this limestone sponge and kept the water from percolating away. Perhaps the two bodies of water were the *joyas*, the jewels, of Salas. Certainly it was their presence that made the little community viable in this arid sector. The water was also the main attraction that had brought us across the mountain; at this time of year, Webster reasoned, the shallow lake and pond were certain to be filled with water birds.

At La Joya we left the trucks and started toward the lake on foot. Right away I had my first field lesson in birding. We were strolling through a dry, stony stretch, sparsely covered with overgrazed grass and acacia. A few small birds flitted through the brush. With an ease and rapidity that was astonishing—even to his fellow birders—Charlie Munn had his tripod-mounted telescope set firmly on the ground and focused on a prospect. "Vermilion flycatcher," he said matter-of-factly, offering me the eyepiece. I recognized the name as one of the minor stars of the Sierra Madre avifauna and for me, a lifer—that is, a species never before seen by the observer. It is not everyone who makes his birding debut by logging so colorful a creature.

Sparrow-sized, the vermilion belongs to the family Tyrannidae, or tyrant flycatchers. There are some 65 members of the family in Mexico, and anyone who can recognize them all is a virtuoso. The male vermilion, however, is easy. Among the tyrant flycatchers—including his dowdy mate—he is a dandy, with bright-red underpinnings and crown, black wings, back and tail. Isolated in Charlie's scope he was a point of fire. And just as the text in Ernest Edwards' guide predicted, we had found him "in rather arid open country," perched "upright" on a mesquite branch, ready to "fly out to catch insects."

Now Jarvis Beverly had focused his binoculars on another bird. We all turned in unison. No question, we were looking at another tyrant flycatcher; the general outline was the same as the vermilion. But the colors were drab—buff on the belly, the rest a dull gray brown. The quandary: was it a male Say's phoebe or a female vermilion? Charlie thought it was a Say's. But the check list that Webster had given us did not include the Say's. It would be a first for the count in this region. Jarvis opted for its being a female vermilion.

While he and Charlie wrangled, I dived into my Edwards. The descriptions of the female vermilion and the Say's phoebe are distressingly alike—so much so that even these experts were at odds on a determination. At that moment Charlie focused on another bird, similar but slightly smaller, perched in the mesquite. This one fit exactly the description of the female flycatcher, which has a blush of pink on the belly. That made the controversial bird a Say's.

Mary made our next score. Though it was also new to the list, Webster had alerted us to this one. "Keep an eye out for a pyrrhuloxia," he cautioned us, "they like the sort of dry scrub you'll find on the other side of the mountain." And there in dry scrub Mary identified a male pyrrhuloxia. It looked like a faded cardinal to me, even to the crested head. Indeed the two are close relatives, with overlapping ranges. The pyrrhuloxia is found in the Southwestern United States and across the border as far south as central Mexico, while the brilliant-red male cardinal occurs throughout the Eastern United States, and over most of Mexico. I wondered how Mary had recognized this bird as a male

These birds are among the 197 species that were identified during author Peter Wood's participation in the 1974-1975 Christmas Bird Count in the Gómez Farías region. Each species was spotted in its favored habitat: the pyrrhuloxia in the arid uplands; the vermilion flycatcher also on dry land but near water; the Altamira oriole in the tropical lowlands; the green jay in the lowlands and the cloud forest; and the blue-hooded euphonia in the cloud forest and wooded uplands.

PYRRHULOXIA

BLUE-HOODED EUPHONIA

VERMILION FLYCATCHER

GREEN JAY

ALTAMIRA ORIOLE

pyrrhuloxia and not a female cardinal. Instead of asking her I leafed through Peterson's guide. It showed the pyrrhuloxia to have a yellow beak, the cardinal a red one, and the body of the female cardinal to be yellow brown, with some reddish tinges on its wings and tail, in contrast to the gray and red of the male pyrrhuloxia. I was learning.

From that fast start the morning wore on interestingly, but without surprises. We spent what was left of it taking a census of water birds, an exercise more dutiful than exciting. Although the primary competition among count areas is the number of different species seen, the more conscientious ornithologists also estimate the number of individual birds seen. By knowing not only what birds are where, but in approximately what numbers at a fixed time each year, preservationists have a bench mark from which to figure migration patterns, to note changing trends and to sound the alarm for endangered species.

The lake was splashed with patches of birds—to my naked eye mere clusters of black dots. Through the scope Charlie was able to break them down into coots, grebes, ruddy ducks, shovelers and a half dozen other water birds. While Jarvis filled his notebook, Charlie scanned the lake, singing out, "eight American widgeon, five gadwalls, eight more American widgeon, twenty pintails, four blue-winged teals, thirteen more pintails," and so on, while the rest of us absorbed the sun and watched a small crew of sandpipers comb the muddy edge of the lake.

When Charlie and Jarvis finished, they had noted 13 species. Almost all were migrants from the north, where nature tends to produce prodigious quantities of a single species—in contrast to the tropics where many different species are represented by relatively few individuals. This particular group of ducks, coots and grebes was an infinitesimal fraction of the millions upon millions of water birds that fly south from Canada and the United States each fall, down the flyways ahead of temperatures that freeze their native lakes, ponds and marshes.

Only a few weeks earlier, 600 miles northwest of the rancho, I had been treated to an early morning view of a typically massive assemblage of such migrants. Some 60 miles southwest of the city of Chihuahua there is a large replica of the little lake at La Joya de Salas. Called Laguna de los Mexicanos, in November and December it fills part of a wide basin with the accumulation of the late summer and fall rains, then dries up slowly during the ensuing six months of sun. There are hundreds of such transitory lakes and marshes on the interior slopes of the two main ranges, and in the central plateau between. The rains

Lesser snow geese arrive for the autumn at Laguna de Guzmán in northwest Mexico after a summer of nesting near the Arctic Circle.

Club mosses line the limestone bed of a stream called Indian Springs, flowing through a glade near Rancho del Cielo.

that fill them each year seem perfectly timed to welcome birds driven down from the north by snow and ice.

When I saw the Laguna de los Mexicanos, it was some five miles long and three miles across. In all directions the basin rolled away beyond the edge of the *laguna*. Some land was in pasture, some in corn and oats; it was the combination of water and grain that brought the birds each year. Shovelers, pintails and teals splashed and quarreled among the reeds near shore and in little satellite ponds. Gliding among them like men o' war amid scruffy harbor boats, great fleets of snow and white-fronted geese and sand-hill cranes made their regal way.

That day, at sunrise, the light was crystalline, the sky a pale luminous blue, the air icy and still. Mountains circled the horizon, and across the whole wide valley birds were moving and calling. They were just finishing a night spent on the lake. Now they rose from it in squadrons, wheeled together, headed toward the fields and settled like a carpet dropped by the wind. While I crouched behind a hedgerow, a flock of sand-hill cranes, among the wariest of the big birds, landed. This bunch numbered 200 or more, and they passed close enough to spot the ones that were calling in their loud trumpeting voices, close enough to count the individual feathers of their gray wing tips and to feel my neck hairs rise at the sound they made as they plowed the air.

After they had passed I stood up and scanned the valley through binoculars, watching the movement and countermovement of the flocks as Napoleon might have surveyed the battle of Austerlitz. There is high emotion in watching so vast a quantity of wildlife on the move. That morning the feeling was intensified—and disturbed—by the knowledge that the guides in Land Rovers who had brought me here had come as antipreservationist spies. This day was a Thursday. On Saturday, having observed the movements and quantities of birds, our drivers would station weekend hunters where they had stationed me. From the very hedgerow where I crouched, men in camouflaged coveralls would stand up and shatter the morning.

Back at La Joya the morning was melting into the heat of midday. To the east white clouds bulged over the ridge line like a layer of meringue. While we were in full sunshine, the rancho, on the eastern slope of the mountain, was smothered in its customary fog and mist. I thought I had been paying close attention to the birds our own team had been spotting. But at the rancho after supper, when the platoons reported, I was amazed to learn that in the few active hours we were in the field we had spotted 34 different bird species. In all, seven platoons (six at the rancho, one at the mountain's base) reported 197 varieties, a total that would be submitted to *American Birds* as our score.

Much later, in New York, I would learn from a visit to Robert Arbib that the official Gómez area count came in at 10th place. The winner was a Mexican Gulf Coast area called Catemaco, which has rain forest as well as a marine environment. To add to that advantage, Catemaco fielded a team of 52 carefully recruited birders, who staked out the area days before the count was made. The result was spectacular. The Catemaco count fell just eight species short of 300.

By contrast, the birders at Rancho del Cielo, though they focused earnestly on the Christmas Bird Count, were fundamentally a crew of hobbyists who stayed around for five subsequent days to revel in the rancho's environment. To me the most interesting of those days was spent walking in a large circle through the cloud forest to the south and southwest of the rancho in the company of a couple named Harms.

Bob Harms, chairman of the Department of Linguistics at the University of Texas, had been birding for only four years. However, this was his second trip to the rancho, and he knew the local birds remarkably well. He and his Finnish-born wife, Sirpa, a botany expert, made agreeable and informative company for Heather, Patrick and me. With us came the rancho caretaker, introduced by Mrs. Warburton simply as Pablo.

At the outer edge of the circle, serving as a destination of sorts, was a place called Indian Springs, about five miles from the rancho. There, a small stream runs out of some rocks sealing a cave in the side of the mountain. We set out along an old logging road that grew narrower and narrower, then petered out in a trail climbing steeply up and to the west. Patrick was constantly disappearing into the undergrowth on either side of the trail. The forest floor was a tumble of limestone boulders and sinkholes. Mrs. Warburton had warned me that although there was no objection to my bringing Patrick, dogs were in some danger in the sierra because of the treacherous topography. He would not be the first dog, she hinted, to disappear, so she suggested keeping him well in hand. That being impossible, I decided to rely on his instincts, however blunted they might be by city life, to keep him out of trouble.

As it turned out, those instincts proved sound. Shortly after we started he flushed a covey of singing quail that flapped off noisily through the trees. Despite their name, the only sound they made was with their wings. Spring and summer—the mating season—are the quails' times

A roadside hawk perched on a stunted tree glares over its shoulder. These small raptors, which never grow to more than 16 inches from head to tail, are named for their habit of perching on fence posts, telegraph poles and wayside trees to scout for their insect, rodent and reptile prey.

to sing. Harms had heard them the last time he was at the rancho, whistling the same notes faster and faster in a furious crescendo. But at any time of year they are timid birds. Without their song to give them away, says one of the bird guides, they are "likely to be overlooked unless accidentally flushed." Score one for dogs.

As we moved deeper into the forest, sun filtered through the canopy, an unusual treat in the cloud forest. During Bob's previous visit, rain had fallen for the entire six days, he told me, with the exception of a few hours one morning. But the rain itself did not bother him; one came prepared for that. Rather it was the dull, color-killing light, since color is the key to the visual identification of birds.

At that moment my eye, casting about in the sun-dappled treetops, caught the red belly and iridescent-green shoulders of a large bird. At last, I thought, a parrot. We all had been looking for parrots, common farther down the mountain, but elusive at the 3,800-foot altitude where we were walking. As a matter of fact, none had been reported by the Rancho del Cielo team on the day of the big count.

"That's no parrot," Bob corrected me. "It's a mountain trogon. Look at its tail." The bird was about the size of an ordinary parrot, but with distinctive tail feathers that jutted down stiffly like the tails of a cutaway coat. Green on the outside, the tail was broadly striped underneath with white and black; in area it was as large as the bird's body. But so well did this bird's tail blend with the sun and shadow in the top of the large sweet gum that I had completely missed it. Now, as Bob pointed it out, the whole bird popped out at me. And a bit to the left of it on a lower branch I saw its mate.

They were the first large tropical birds I had seen in Mexico. As they sat and watched us out of big, round eyes, I felt I had stepped at last across the threshold of this mountain wilderness. When we moved closer they took off, flying heavily through the treetops. Bob told me these mountain trogons were close relatives of the quetzal.

As we reached the height of the ridge our way led between rocky piles of limestone heaped like gigantic ruins, covered in vines and mosses, the whole somberly topped by a closed canopy of trees. We passed inviting grottoes and large brush-filled pits formed when the roofs of underground caverns fell in. Suddenly, out of a large depression on our left, a blackish-brown, turkey-sized bird with a bushy crest flew up into a giant maple. Then another went up, and another and another. Crashing after them in hopeless earth-bound pursuit was Patrick.

"Guan," cried Bob and Pablo simultaneously. The crested guan and a related species called the great curassow are among the prime game birds of the sierra forests. The guan can be found on coastal slopes of both the Occidental and Oriental ranges, the curassow mainly on the coastal slopes of the Oriental. Both birds are arboreal, but scratch in the ground for acorns in winter—as these guans had probably been doing when Patrick jumped them. For several days they had been heard around the rancho. Their characteristic cackles and honks had been sufficient identification for them to have been included in the Christmas Bird Count. But until now none of us had seen one. We would probably have walked right by them had Patrick not been working the brush. The guans put on quite a show as they moved through the treetops; and then, before I could really register it all, they were gone.

We stood quite breathless, trying to savor what we had seen. But it had all happened so quickly that it was hard to reconstruct. Someone more accustomed than I to the sight of guans could put it together —someone, for instance, like George Miksch Sutton, an ornithologist and illustrator who had been one of the first birders in the Gómez area. In 1941 Sutton spent several weeks at the base of the mountain and chronicled the experience in a book called *At a Bend in a Mexican River*. There one day he had "watched a pair of crested guans racing nonchalantly forty to sixty feet above ground, leaping from one branch to another without so much as lifting a wing . . . slipping with serpentine effortlessness along the branches, swinging their big tails from side to side to keep their balance." Though they were at times obscured by the foliage, he had never lost "sight of their glowing red throat wattles," a feature I had overlooked entirely. "Finally," says Sutton's text, "flying to a dead tree and running and hopping to the very top, they stood quietly not far apart, as if contemplating the sky." With Patrick barking at them, our guans had spent no time in contemplation.

The curly crested great curassow—which, alas, we did not see—is an odd member of the avian world in that the female is somewhat flashier than the male, her unusual black-and-white-checkered head and throat more distinctive than his yellow-knobbed black head.

My notes list dozens of other birds on the way to the spring and along the long, looping trail we took back. Among them were the acorn woodpecker, so called for its favorite food, which it pounds into holes in a tree, possibly against times of lean feeding; the least pygmy-owl, small and tawny brown with a high-pitched whistle; and the squirrel cuckoo, bright cinnamon with a long tail. Bob Harms called up a number of birds by imitating the trilling whistle of the screech owl. The owl is the natural enemy of all little forest birds—but rather than run from its sound they are attracted to it, possibly to keep the enemy in sight. That night Bob Harms could announce that he had seen three lifers. As for me, most sightings were so brief they blurred in my mind.

One sighting did not. Bob had pointed the bird out to me, high in the top of an old oak, feeding on mistletoe berries. The hour was late and the sun slanted obliquely into the treetop, lighting it like a stage. High up and in clear view was a sole performer, a blue-hooded euphonia —lovely bird, lovely name. Through binoculars that brought it seemingly within reach, we watched for many minutes while the euphonia flitted back and forth, hovering under the hanging berries, plucking one, then darting to a perch to swallow it. The crown and nape of its neck were bright blue, its upper parts a deep, glossy blackish purple. This bird, like the guan and trogon, belongs to the tropical forest. And I felt, somehow, that the sight of it belonged to me.

On our final day, after breakfast, the trucks were scheduled to take all the birders down the mountain again. Rather than submit to the beating I had taken coming up, I consigned my baggage to a truck and set out on foot with the Harmses. We had a head start and it would be an hour or so before the truck caught up with us. A thousand feet down the mountain we saw our first parrots, chattering noisily in the top of a dead tree. As usual, Bob Harms came to my assistance. "Red-lored parrots," he told me. "See the red patch above the beak."

In the village of Gómez two hours later, there was a flurry of goodbyes as we separated into our various cars. A mile or two below the village Heather and I spotted a large predatory bird sitting on a fence. I stopped the car and grabbed my binoculars. Suspecting what it was, I told Heather to turn to the appropriate page in Peterson.

While I kept my eye on the bird, Heather read: "Gray brown, rufous barring on underparts." Yes. "Rufous primaries. Tail banded with pale gray and dark brown." Yes. "Habitat—roadsides, woodland borders; mainly lower elevations." Yes, again.

No doubt about it, the bird was a roadside hawk. My first untutored identification—and a lifer, at that.

A Glorious Botanical Confusion

Although the college research station known as Rancho del Cielo near Gómez Farías, Mexico, has recently become renowned as an ornithologist's paradise, it was first established as a preserve for the region's enormous—and anomalous—variety of plants. In fact the same environmental factors that draw the birds have also encouraged the development of a cornucopia of plants.

The rancho benefits broadly from its location on one side of a corridor between two vastly different continents. Here it is in position to play host to growing things from both. But although basic geography is one key to the creation of the rancho's plant treasury, the extraordinary variances in local topography and weather exert equal influences. The rancho perches on the eastern flank of the Sierra de Guatemala, a subrange of the Sierra Madre Oriental, 90 miles inland from the Gulf of Mexico. Warm, wet winds sliding in from the Gulf climb the side of the sierra, dumping moisture as they go. At the base of the range, 25 to 60 inches fall per year. In the middle is a moist zone that receives 140 inches. At the top and just beyond the crest, the clouds are spent and plants compete for a sparse 20 inches.

The vegetation varies accordingly; within each zone are natives as well as adaptable immigrants from other climes and lands. At the foot of the mountains is a combination of tropical deciduous forests. In the middle zone, as part of a luxuriant cloud forest, the sweet gum of New England flourishes side by side with the red-berried eugenia of Costa Rica. And over the high ridge line the oaks of a temperate forest are entwined by tropical orchids.

Among the questions botanists are trying to answer is how this unusual combination of species occurred in the first place. One theory holds that seeds may have spread overland at a time when all the continents were connected and the whole earth enjoyed a mild climate. Another theory suggests that heat-loving plants from the north retreated to warm, humid pockets in these mountains when a glacial period drove them out of their homes. A third explanation is that migratory birds and atmospheric winds carried seeds into the area. However it happened, the Rancho del Cielo region and the cloud forest in particular remain as an intriguingly beautiful spot, where both endemic plants and former strangers dwell in glorious botanical confusion.

A fan palm (top) and a shagbark hickory (bottom) share the moist forest soil. The fan palm is a rare tropical species exclusive to eastern Mexico; the hickory's normal range is the Eastern United States and Quebec. The fernlike plant between them is a member of the ubiquitous pea family.

A sprig of tropical croton shrub sprouts white male and green female flowers.

Bignonia, a woody climbing vine, reaches maturity in a spray of pink blossoms.

A Forest within a Forest

In the mountains near Rancho del Cielo, the lowest life zone—extending from about 250 feet to 1,800 feet above sea level—contains two different tropical forests.

From one, bombax and acacia trees draped with bromeliads rise out of a dense understory of prickly cactus, croton shrubs and woody vines *(left)*. In the dry winter season, when the trees shed their leaves, they are virtually indistinguishable from trees of the tropical deciduous forests farther south in Mexico and Central America.

Within this dominant forest, much of whose rain water seeps away through its limestone underpinnings, lies a second, quite different forest. This one thrives along the banks of two streams that course through the lowlands, the Río Frio and Río Sabinas *(right)*. Here the plants are a fascinating mixture of water-loving figs and cypresses whose relatives range far south, and willows and sycamores whose relatives appear far into the north. Unlike the deciduous trees of the larger forest surrounding them, the moisture seekers either keep their leaves year-round or lose them so briefly that they form a permanent green ribbon along the stream banks.

The broad bases of two Montezuma bald cypresses stand awash in the Río Sabinas during a season of unusually intense rain. Adapted to riverside living and periodic flooding, such trees sometimes survive for over 1,000 years.

A Botanical Kingdom in a Cloud

The lushest vegetation on the east wall of these mountains grows in its moist middle zone 2,200 to 5,500 feet above sea level. At the very center of this zone lies America's northernmost cloud forest, a 1,500-acre wilderness tract in which both tropical and temperate plants intermingle.

Each year the cloud forest is drenched by six months of rain, beginning in late May and tapering down in late October. During this wet season, the forest is usually veiled in mist. Even in dry months intermittent showers assure enough humidity so that trees, shrubs, mosses, vines and flowers flourish to an awesome degree.

Dahlias shoot up to 15 feet; more than three dozen orchid species thrive (overleaf). Though crowded and festooned with epiphytes, the trees—the tallest in the range—grow to 100 feet. Four sugar-maple species occur here—twice the number found in the New England woods with which they are commonly linked.

But the greatest wonder of the cloud forest is its even-handed hospitality. Living side by side are maple and *Podocarpus*, sweet gum and *Cedrela*, hickory and palm, and a host of other plants that more often grow thousands of miles apart.

Blurred by a low-hanging haze, oaks and sweet gums rise out of the cloud-forest understory. The shrubs in the foreground—all natives—are, from left, a Humboldt butterfly bush, a poisonous mala mujer and a scarlet runner bean.

SERPENT HEAD

These six species of orchid are among the 40 that thrive in and around the cloud forest, an unusual total for so small an area this far north of the equator. Of those shown here—some so rare they lack common names—the serpent head, hyacinth and clamshell are epiphytes, or air plants, living aloft on trees, taking nourishment from rain, dust and air. The rest root in the soil.

MALAXIS

GOVENIA

HYACINTH ORCHID

CRYBE

CLAMSHELL ORCHID

A Mexican sugar maple with new red leaves and a pale-leafed sweet gum (left), sprout beneath a mature tropical Podocarpus tree.

An epiphytic Rhipsalis cactus hangs in streamers from a tree.   *A parasite called love vine entwines an unresisting buckthorn shrub.*

This sampling of brilliant flowering plants of the moist zone includes three shrubs (directly below) and seven wild flowers. The Louteridium and Zephyranthes are found only in this region. Sweet laurel has a close relative 1,000 miles northeast in the United States and another in China.

SWEET LAUREL

TRINITY PLANT

LOUTERIDIUM

TURK'S CAP

DAHLIA

WILD POINSETTIA

ZEPHYRANTHES

ARTHROSTEMMA

TIGER APPLE

TAGETES

Dry Enclave in a Moist Range

Just over the 8,000-foot crest of the range, in the rain shadow of the easterlies, stands a dry forest dotted with pines and oaks. The vegetation is more sparsely distributed than in the cloud forest across the ridge and farther down the slopes. Moreover, the trees here are shorter than their relatives in the moist zone. The oaks, for example, grow stunted and gnarled, with spreading crowns; like other species in this dry enclave, most of them are well under 80 feet.

Yet even here there are touches of the tropics. Although the richer growth of epiphytes and lianas that flourish in the wet areas is absent, orchids, ferns and Spanish mosses bedeck many trees and deep-pink rain lilies burst into bloom.

Twisted oaks and slender pines form a backdrop for a gallery of plants. In the left foreground is the spiny agave, normally a desert dweller; at the right, yellow-flowered Wedelia grow atop a jagged limestone outcrop. And in the right background are three examples of a rare endemic plant of this unique mountain habitat —bayonet-leafed Nolina nelsonii.

4/ An Ocean of Mountains

For once they would learn what a really tough trail on the Sierra Madre is like when hell and heaven are against the traveller.

B. TRAVEN/ *THE TREASURE OF THE SIERRA MADRE*

Strangers do not walk lightly into the Sierra Madre Occidental—not Humphrey Bogart looking for gold nor a writer simply seeking untrammeled wilderness. The Grand Sierra, as it is aptly called by people who know it, is only haphazardly mapped; there are no forest rangers, no signs to guide the hiker. The weight of the unknown bears down on him, and like a backpack that may have seemed inconsequential in the cool of morning, it grows heavier with every hour, every step.

Prudently, I took my first look at the Occidental from the air. As the plane flew westward from the city of Chihuahua on Mexico's high central plateau, the first sight of the range was reassuring. Its eastern slopes rise gently from the plateau, and are mantled by oak and pine. Farther on along the very spine of the mountains, there are large areas of savanna—a great natural highway that has been used by animals and men migrating north and south since prehistoric times. I was beginning to feel a measure of self-confidence—until the western half of the range hove into view. Here the understructure of long-hardened lava and volcanic ash that lies hidden beneath the grass and forests of the eastern half is revealed in all its formidable complexity. The mountains are gashed by precipitously plunging canyons, some more than a mile deep. I had heard of these colossal clefts in the earth—the barrancas—and I had every intention of exploring one. But as I looked straight down into them from the plane, I knew I would need some prior toughening.

As we were flying back to Chihuahua over the dry, dun-colored central plain, I decided to do some rehearsing before I entered the Occidental. Ahead of us, abruptly jutting out of the desert, I saw a mountain range that was a small, concentrated version of the Grand Sierra. It appeared to be only about 20 miles long and less than 10 miles wide—in contrast to the Occidental's 750-mile length and 100-mile breadth—and it did not look unduly challenging. This pocket-sized cordillera would be a perfect place to practice. To cross it, I calculated, would take an easy four-day jaunt. The name of the range, the pilot informed me, was the Sierra del Nido.

Caution suggested, however, that I not try to do it alone. In Chihuahua I joined forces with Dick Phelan, whom a mutual friend had recommended as a knowledgeable Sierra Madre veteran and an amiable companion for my trip into the Occidental. Dick, a Texan, was currently writing a book about his home state's natural history; he agreed to take time off for the Sierra del Nido adventure. As things turned out, Dick's assets as a wilderness companion included one highly unusual gift. He could recite poetry, from Longfellow to Dorothy Parker, for hours on end, and it took only a small nudge to set him off.

On a day in early December, shortly after sunrise, a Mexican bush pilot dropped the two of us in a field in the western hills of El Nido. As the plane's wheels touched down, an animal the size of a big bulldog leaped high out of the grass—a bobcat. After one look at us from cold eyes above a square, whiskered jaw, it disappeared into a thicket of dark-green juniper. Minutes later, with a roar and a rush of air, the four-seat Cessna taxied for a takeoff. Dick and I were alone in icy stillness. The field lay in shadow, covered with hoarfrost. We put on more clothes, shouldered our packs, cinched the hip straps and started walking into the range.

Topographically, the Sierra del Nido is a reverse image of the Occidental. Its gentler slopes are found on the western side; its highest and steepest wall is on the east. Our plan consisted of making our way in from the west, then proceeding up and across the main ridge to the eastern wall. Then, from there, we would descend to the desert floor abutting the escarpment.

The canyon slope we began to climb, following the course of a small stream, offered no difficulties. The arroyo was dotted with madrones, some of the handsomest trees I had ever seen, with smooth-barked trunks and glossy, rhododenron-like leaves. As we walked, we talked of our chances of seeing a more elusive occupant of El Nido: *oso pla-*

teado, the grizzly bear or silvertip. Once plentiful throughout the Sierra Madre, this subspecies of *Ursus horribilis,* to use its expressive Latin name, is well on its way to disappearing from Mexico's mountains. But a silvertip had been shot in the Sierra del Nido in 1968, and I had talked to a deer hunter in Chihuahua who claimed to have sighted one there as recently as two years ago. Take a rifle, he had warned—if not for the bear, then for the wolves and *el tigre,* as Mexicans call the jaguar. But that was not the sort of expedition Dick and I had in mind.

We camped that night on a grassy flat at a fork in the canyon. Our first day had been easy, and somehow I felt that the other three days would not be much harder. But in the morning the first faint hint of trouble appeared. The stream we had followed into the range had played out, and we would need water if we were to go on. Dick and I left our tent and packs and set out separately to explore the canyon's arms.

I had barely swung out of sight of our camp before I startled a white-tailed deer. Later I came upon a dozen more of them browsing in a little clearing; they bounded away like porpoises. After a couple of hours, my arm of the canyon led up onto a high savanna, which supported pines and oaks at wide intervals, like an English park. From here I could see peaks several miles eastward—the main ridge. But ahead of me lay a far deeper canyon than the one we had come up. To reach the main ridge I would have to swing in a wide arc to the north around the head of this obstacle.

The savanna soon narrowed to an apex of weathered rock. Here, where the mountain was laid bare to the bone, great columnar boulders covered with moss leaned against one another or lay heavily on their sides. A deer trail picked its way through the maze. I followed, crossing several more cols and hills until I judged—I had no watch—that half of the day was gone. I would have to turn back. Rather than retracing my up-and-down course, I decided to skirt around a shoulder of one of the hills. An hour later I realized I was lost—or if not lost, at least not where I reckoned I ought to be. I had a choice. I could either retrace my steps and thereby lose two hours and any chance to reach camp by dark; or I could reassess my position and set a new course forward. I had matches, so I could build a fire to survive the freezing cold that night, but I had only a ski jacket for warmth and nothing to eat or drink, for I had found no water.

Suddenly and unthinkingly, I began to run in the direction I was pointed, leaping over fallen logs, smashing through underbrush. Stupid, I knew. If I twisted or broke an ankle I would be in real trouble. Moreover, if I was headed the right way I had no need to run. And if I was headed wrong I was only compounding my error. But I continued on clumsily in the heavy hiking boots as fast as I could go. Then, on a slope ahead of me, I saw a single deer. This one did not see me. The fact that it had not heard my thunderous progress can only have been some acoustical quirk of the terrain. I stopped and crept slowly forward to within 50 feet of the buck before it raised its head in alarm and fled. I came to my senses then and began walking more carefully and observantly. About 15 minutes later I reached the columnar rocks. I was back on course with plenty of time to reach camp before dark.

I propped myself in a natural seat among the boulders. It was the first time I had sat down since morning. The sun was warm. The only sound was a slight breeze pushing through the pine tops. In a few minutes a foot-long coal-black lizard slithered out onto a rock, spotted me and froze. Then, literally in the blink of my eye, it was gone. I had expected El Nido's reptiles, being cold-blooded creatures, to be dormant at this time of year. Though the cordillera is noted for its population of rattlesnakes, particularly the red-and-white-patterned species called the Willard's rattler, I had given little thought to watching out for snakes. Now I began to wonder. It occurred to me that while the weather had been freezing the night before in our camp some 1,000 feet below, the temperature by now was at least 50° higher—enough of a swing to make a lizard, and its fellow reptiles, pretty lively.

A slight movement around a nearby stagbush caught my eye. Blue butterflies no bigger than dimes, a dozen of them, hovered around the white blossoms of the bush. These delicate insects have their own means of dealing with sharp temperature fluctuations. The fluid that flows through their systems works something like antifreeze. During cold nights, the butterflies fall into a torpor, but with the warmth of the sun they are soon off with all their flighty energy.

I was still contemplating the bush and its pollinators when I heard a shuffling sound from the other side of a boulder. This ridge I was on was a natural road. I held my breath. *Ursus horribilis?* Dick's head appeared around the boulder. His way up onto the savanna had been less direct than mine, but an easier climb. Better yet, a quarter mile above our camp he had found a deep pool of water. We would be able to start with full canteens in the morning.

By 11:30 the next day we were back again at the rocky ridge. This time, under the full weight of our packs, we stepped slowly and deliberately. By early afternoon we reached the base of a butte that marked my farthest exploration of the day before. We decided to skirt it, aiming for a slightly lower prominence farther on. On its north slope, we ate a late lunch in a shadowy grove of tall Douglas firs, perhaps the remnants of a great forest that covered these mountains during the last ice age over 12,000 years ago.

There were no man-made trails at all; we had to pick our way over windfalls, small arroyos and scree. Not until late afternoon did we finally reach a point from which we could look down the eastern flank of El Nido and out across the desert. What we saw was not encouraging. None of the canyons ahead of us promised a sure exit to the east; worse, they appeared dry. We had only enough water left for supper and perhaps for coffee the next morning. No doubt there were springs and seeps in some of the canyons—but in which ones?

To avoid finishing the hike bone dry, we needed to find a trail with water along it somewhere. We agreed to stay where we were for the night, picking a sheltered spot to camp. We knew it might be windy here on top, and it certainly would be far colder than our previous camp, for we were now a mile and a half above sea level. Meanwhile, I would use the last light of day to work my way along the ridge looking for a trail—dry or no—down the far side.

After a time I came upon a complex of old logging tracks that started down the eastern side. I let out a whoop of joy—prematurely. I followed each spur in turn, but all of them ended abruptly where the land pitched too steeply for men to handle the timber. Obviously the logging tracks had been made by crews coming in from the west. By following these blind leads, therefore, I was lured a good distance away from the point where I had left Dick. I stood there in the fading light, sweaty, cold, exhausted, looking out over the roughest piece of country I ever encountered.

The sun had set at my back. I was facing east into shadow. The sky, deep blue at the zenith, graded to a gray opalescence at the horizon. The desert floor, more than a mile below me, was dark purple and featureless. In the foreground the muscular shoulders of the cordillera rose up, flexed into a confusion of interconnecting creases. At my feet the earth—tufted in dry, yellow grasses, dark now and forbidding under a canopy of pine—pitched away, steep as a dam face.

I turned to retrace my steps, then began once again to run, afraid darkness might overtake me. The air is so pure in these mountains that

Congealed mist coats a dense forest of pines, oaks and manzanita shrubs on top of the hump-backed main ridge of the Sierra del Nido.

the particles that catch and reflect the sun's afterglow are scant, and night comes frighteningly fast. I kept running until I saw the bright blue of my backpack where I had left it against a gnarled and stunted madrone only about three feet high. Then, slightly below the ridge line, I spotted a second bright dab of color, a campfire. Dick had been busy. My anxiety diminished, but not my sense of frustration.

Over supper we debated what to do. Our failure to spot a grizzly could not be taken as too serious a disappointment. But what I had set my heart on was crossing this runt of a range. We could stretch our food for two days more, but after tomorrow morning we would be out of water. There was no use looking for it on the top of the mountain and there was no certainty of there being any on the dry eastern side.

Nothing to debate, Dick pointed out. With no trail it would be foolish to plunge ahead. Reluctantly, I had to agree.

The next morning the issue was settled conclusively. A heavy fog lay on the mountain. Visibility was a bare 30 feet. But what a 30 feet! The fog, drifting up from the east during the night, had frozen on every leaf, needle, twig and blade—not like the shellac of freezing rain but as a border of silver lace along each leading edge. I have seen the aftermath of ice storms sparkling in the sun, a cruel beauty that bends and shatters. This arrangement was so delicate, so gentle that I was tempted not to move for fear of destroying the crystals.

Practicality soon shattered that romantic notion. We shook the bushes over my poncho, collecting piles of fluffy ice, which we then melted in a pot. With plenty of water now, we could have continued to look for a way east if only the fog lifted. Instead it grew thicker. And through it came ominous rolls of thunder. Sudden winter storms sometimes sweep through these mountains, sending the temperature plunging 40° in as many minutes. We hurriedly packed and made our way to the westward-leading logging road I had found the evening before.

Twelve hours later, stumbling with fatigue, we entered a farmyard in the valley west of El Nido. The storm had pursued us down the mountain. Emerging from the last arroyo onto the plain late in the day, we searched the distance with Dick's field glasses and saw a low cluster of buildings. A Mennonite settlement, Dick guessed. A group of these Evangelical Protestants had come from Canada to colonize this valley in the 1920s. Rather than make camp out in the open under the threatening clouds, we decided to keep on. For the next two hours we trudged in inky darkness, aiming at a pin point of light that turned out to be a bare electric bulb mounted on the side of a large hay barn.

We slept on the wooden floor of a Mennonite farmhouse that night. Breakfast came early—huge bowls of steaming oatmeal, thick farm bread, butter, coffee. Warm and full, I stepped out of doors. A light dusting of snow covered the barnyard mud. Way in the distance—had we really walked that far?—the Sierra del Nido jutted up against the eastern horizon. A thin strip of orange sky was squeezed between the ridge top and a low layer of clouds. There would be no fog, then, on the mountain this morning.

But it was too late to go back. Dick and I had an appointment farther west, in the Grand Sierra. And this time we planned to take a guide. Two guides, in fact—one directing us from beyond the grave.

In searching the meager literature of the Sierra Madre with an eye to learning something of its natural history, I had very soon come upon the name Carl Lumholtz. During the 1890s, Lumholtz, a Norwegian theology student turned naturalist, explorer and anthropologist, spent five years traversing the entire length of Mexico's massive western cordillera. Nothing written about the Grand Sierra before or since matches the scope of his report, entitled *Unknown Mexico*.

At one stage of his journey, in January of 1892, Lumholtz stopped at Chuhuichupa, then a small settlement in a shallow upland valley in the northern Occidental. There he hired an old Mexican soldier who had been recommended as a man who knew the Sierra Madre better than anyone. The man's name was Don Teodoro. With him as guide, the caravan moved southward over an ancient trail into mountain country "so wild and rugged that the greatest care had to be exercised with the animals, lest one of them tumble to his death down the near-vertical slopes. Some 8,200 feet up, at a promontory that Don Teodoro called Punto Magnifico, Lumholtz beheld a glorious view of peak after peak stretching away into limitless distance. He likened the sight to "an ocean of mountains."

Though Lumholtz found a country largely empty of man, it was not without signs of past human tenancy. Beyond Punto Magnifico, Don Teodoro led the expedition into a deep canyon called Arroyo de Guaynopa. "While zigzagging our way down," Lumholtz wrote, "we caught sight of a large cave with houses and some white cone-shaped structures staring at us across an arroyo."

The cones turned out to be food storage vats, the houses the dwellings of a large group of Indians. Along their way the travelers found other caves that contained dozens of rooms constructed out of adobe mud, stones and wattle. These caves, quite different from the limestone caverns of the eastern sierra, were wide, shallow openings in the canyon faces. Everywhere Lumholtz found *trincheras,* stone retaining walls built by ancient generations of mountain dwellers to slow and divert water on the slopes and to make small terraces for planting crops. But the builders of this hidden civilization had long since departed when Lumholtz arrived.

If the country was without people when Lumholtz got there, it nonetheless teemed with animal life. "Never have I been at any place where deer were more plentiful," he marveled. In mid-January, with snow on the ground, he found "a multitude of green parrots with pretty red and yellow heads chattering in the tree tops and feasting on pine cones." He described with awe "*Campephilus imperialis,* the largest woodpecker in the world." Lumholtz was not exaggerating. With a body length of 20 to 22 inches, this splendid scarlet-crested bird, found only in the Grand Sierra and now dangerously close to extinction, is the giant of all the world's 209 woodpecker species.

Not much has changed in the northern Grand Sierra since Lumholtz saw it. A growing lumber industry has cut down trees on the most accessible slopes and slaughtered game to feed the workers. Many of the cave sites have been measured by archeologists and carefully excavated, and the results have been embalmed in scholarly papers. But despite such invasions, the country remains as formidable as Lumholtz described it. Dick and I decided we would try to follow part of his trail into the Grand Sierra. We particularly wanted to find the cave at Guaynopa, which seems to have attracted little attention from the world of academe.

Arrangements were not easy. In the end they were accomplished only with the help of the Mexican government, through an agency based in Chihuahua and called Profortarah, for Productos Forestales de los Tarahumara. The *productos* are pulp and lumber; the Tarahumara are the major surviving tribe of Grand Sierra indigenes. A shy, retiring people, numbering some 50,000, they once lived in the northern part of the range, but now are chiefly settled farther south.

A surveyor with Profortarah offered enthusiastically to help. He loaned us a truck and a driver to make the 150-mile journey fom Chihuahua to Mesa del Hurracan, a lumber mill and company town set down in the northern sierra heights, and not very far from Chuhuichupa, the jumping-off point Lumholtz had used to get to the caves.

At Mesa del Hurracan we picked up our guide—a firewarden for the lumber agency who, the surveyor had assured us, "knew the area like the back of his hand." He was short, barrel chested, bowlegged, with a white mustache, a large handsome nose, strong black eyes and a perfect set of white teeth. He was not a former soldier, like Lumholtz' guide, but he was old—71 years old, he later told us—and his name was Teodolo. Naturally we called him Don Teodolo.

Did he know the cave in Guaynopa? Of course! And the trail down into the canyon? *Si, señor!* But such a trip would take at least four days —two down and two back. And we would need mules. Only a very poor Tarahumara or a madman would carry his own gear in this country. Why else did the good Lord invent mules?

How long to arrange for mules? A day, two days, possibly more. *Quien sabe?*

Impossible, we countered. Our truck and driver were expected back in Chihuahua long before that. There must be some other way.

Bueno, said Teodolo, there is another possibility. We could approach from the side of the arroyo that the cave is on. That way we would not have to go all the way to the bottom and climb up again. And our truck could carry us over a logging road to within a three-hour walk of the cave. We could leave that very morning and be back the next evening. Right, we said, let's go.

We would not need the tent, Teodolo assured us; the cave was warm and protected. So Dick and I lightened our loads to include no more than a full change of clothes, sleeping bags, freeze-dried trail food, knives, cameras, snakebite kits, extra socks, canteens, and halizone tablets for the dirty water. All of which made us feel a mite foolish when Teodolo reappeared 15 minutes later all set to go. His only preparation had been to change into a pair of black basketball sneakers and to acquire a paper bag full of tortillas. He carried no pack and was dressed simply in a wool shirt over a cotton shirt, chinos and, of course, the straw hat without which no sane male in these parts would put his head out of doors, even to spit.

The drive to the head of the logging road took several hours, first through high, flat savanna, then into much more difficult terrain as the land fell away toward the western watershed of the sierra. Arroyos whose depths were invisible to us undulated up to ridges lit up by the sun, the pattern repeating itself but growing bluer and dimmer in the distance. And nowhere in that enormous panorama was there any visible sign of man. I understood now what Lumholtz had meant by the words "an ocean of mountains." The immensity of the expanse generated within me the same strong emotions of fright and exaltation that I feel when viewing the sea.

Around midday, the road started down the side of an arroyo, then ended abruptly when the pitch of the slope became too steep. From here we would have to continue on foot. We took some time out to eat lunch by the side of the truck—no use carrying an extra ounce. In any event, we were in no great hurry; it was only a three-hour hike to the cave, Teodolo repeated.

Dick and I laced up our hiking boots, shouldered our packs and, having arranged to meet the truck at the same spot the next afternoon, stepped off the road and down the steep, forested side of the ravine. Teodolo led the way. As we descended we came upon a little stream of crystal-clear water. The pine and juniper trees around us were enormous. Two men facing each other could hardly have joined hands around the great trunks that rose 50 to 60 feet before branching. No loggers had been down here; no road could possibly have been built to reach this place.

There was a lushness to the ravine that increased as we followed the course of the stream lower and lower. Sycamores, oaks and other deciduous trees were now mixed in with the junipers and pines. Dried leaves carpeted the ground; the sun grew warm and the feeling was of an Indian-summer afternoon in a New England forest. We passed deep, inviting pools of water and brief cascades tumbling over mossy rocks; with each drop the stream grew in size. By 3:30 in the afternoon Dick and I began to look around hopefully for the cave. But just about that time Teodolo crossed to the far side of the stream and began to follow a mule trail up the opposite slope.

As we left the stream behind, the character of the terrain changed. The vegetation was soon thorny and scrubby. Cactus, agave and acacia replaced the deep forest glades. Soon, Teodolo told us, we would reach Arroyo de Guaynopa. But the trail grew fainter and fainter, and sometime during the next hour it dawned on us that this was a part of the back of Teodolo's hand that he had not scrutinized for some time. We put the question bluntly to him. It had been 10 years, he admitted, since he had last visited the cave, and then he had come another way, so he had been able to spot its gaping mouth from a distance. To us, approaching from behind and above, the cave would be invisible. Teodolo was certain that it was somewhere below us, but he was not sure ex-

Tenanted in centuries past by Chichimec Indians, a cave in the Arroyo de Guaynopa retains traces of dwellings and grain storage bins.

actly at what point to start the descent. So we trudged on, and finally arrived at the rim of a canyon—Guaynopa. Five hours had passed since we had left the truck.

Only then did I realize why this route, which had seemed so direct at the time Teodolo first described it, was really so difficult. Imagine a many-legged creature, a centipede perhaps, and yourself a mite en route from its head to its tail. A course down the middle of the insect's back, even if it were twisted and bent as much as this country was, would make comparatively smooth going. Now, however, conceive of a parallel course, but this time leading along one flank of the centipede. You must make your way up over one leg, then down into the hollow between it and the next, up over the next leg and so forth until either exhaustion or night overtakes you.

It was over this maddening route that the stiff-legged but indefatigable Teodolo led us. He had told us that there was a good spring close to the cave, so naturally no one had bothered to fill up the canteens at the stream. All of us were hot, tired and thirsty. When the sun went down, Teodolo decided that it was time, willy-nilly, to descend into the canyon. We picked our way gingerly down through acacia thickets and Spanish bayonet that disputed our passage. Finally we arrived at a cattle trail and Teodolo took heart. Only a half hour or more down the canyon, he informed us, we would come upon the spring, and then above it the cave.

But we did not have a half hour of light left. When we came to a clearing in the forest where a large oak had fallen, it was nearly black night and suddenly very cold. Dick and I had our sleeping bags, but Teodolo had nothing except the clothes he wore to keep him warm. A fire, we reasoned, was more important than water, and the oak tree provided ample wood. So we settled down, ate a dry meal and built a roaring bonfire. Teodolo curled up as close to it as he dared with my ski jacket under him. (Too close, as a hole in my jacket later attested.) Every 20 minutes or so, he turned himself like a hot dog roasting on a stick, and in the morning he seemed none the worse for temperatures that must have approached freezing.

With first light, we continued to follow the cattle trail to the spring, a little trickle of warm water that oozed out from under a mossy boulder. The black mud around it was heavily trampled by cattle that roam semi-wild through these hills. Teodolo crouched and drank right out of a little pool that had formed in a hoofprint. But we filled our canteens instead, as always careful to dose the contents with halizone. From our first day in El Nido, Dick had been adamant about this precaution. Even here, where there were no people to pollute the water, the cattle did the job. Those who had lived all their lives in these parts, like Teodolo, could tolerate the high count of toxic bacteria in the water. We could not. Thirsty as we were, therefore, we waited 22 minutes, by Dick's watch, for the halizone to do its bacteria-killing work. And that is about how long it took us to find the cave.

The cave was above the spring, Teodolo assured us, so we began to climb again. We came first to several of the ancient retaining walls, the *trincheras.* The low piles of stones were so overgrown with grass and mosses that I would never have noticed them had not Teodolo pointed them out to us as works of *los antiguos.*

We began to scramble up the slope, broke through a tangle of dense underbrush and a maze of fallen boulders. Suddenly, there above us, loomed the cave. I was totally unprepared for what we saw. Because we had come from below, the opening—fully 200 feet wide and 40 feet high—had been hidden until we were actually standing on the very lip.

Awed into silence, the three of us began to prowl around. The ceiling of the cave sloped back to meet the floor at a point some 60 feet inside. Water had probably run through the cave at one time, flushing out a softer underlayer of rock and leaving a vaulted roof of more durable stuff. Now the floor was dust dry, and inside the great dim space there was a sterile, tomblike quiet. The remains of a cluster of low, dark rooms made of plastered mud and stones hugged the back wall of the cave. Another group of rooms, built into two stories, filled the right-hand corner. They averaged about 12 feet square; some had small niches in the walls. The doors were curiously shaped like a wide, squared-off T, as if to fit a big, squat key.

Shards of red and black pottery and tatters of woven baskets lay about. I noticed a number of hand-worn pieces of wood that looked as though they might have served as tool handles. There were several *metates,* the concave stones in which the Indians—as well as present-day Mexican peasants—ground their corn. Most were smashed, but one was in perfect shape. It must have weighed at least 60 pounds, which is probably why it was still there. The place had obviously been raked long ago for its more portable artifacts such as scrapers and axes, for which there was a market in the outside world.

The most interesting structures still left were the remains of several granaries—the "cone-shaped structures" near the entrance that Lumholtz had described. They had been used to store corn and beans, and though empty now, two of them were largely intact. Essentially they were mammoth jars, standing about eight feet tall. They had been built by coiling up grasses and plastering them with mud; when filled to the top the jars had been sealed to protect the contents from rodents. On the floor of the cave I noticed a few thumb-sized corncobs, clean as old bones. I picked one up and ran my fingers over the rough surface; I could not tell whether the tiny cob was simply the immature corn sometimes picked and eaten by local Indians today, or whether it was a runty ancestor of modern corn—buried until very recently under cave debris—that had been used by the families who built these apartments and storage jars some 900 years ago.

The history of these people has been pieced together by anthropologists working at cave sites like Guaynopa and at the ruins of a city at the edge of the Grand Sierra 75 miles to the northeast. The Aztecs, who controlled the country to the south, called the people living in these mountains Chichimecs—"sons of dogs" or, roughly, barbarians. Compared to the Aztecs, the Chichimecs were indeed crude. But their culture, too, flourished for a brief period. The evidence lies in the remains of their city, which Spanish colonizers later named Casas Grandes—the Big Houses.

By the mid-16th Century, when the Spaniards arrived, the city was already in ruins, and the local Indians could account for its origins only in a vague legend. But its past splendor was traceable in the dimensions of its homes and public places and in the sophistication of its engineering, which included underground water ducts and an effective air-conditioning system based on designing and placing doors and windows so as to create drafts. The city had been built rapidly, in a kind of construction boom around the year 1060. For 280 years it was a thriving center of trade and agriculture. Then, in 1340, it was either sacked or abandoned or both. People died in the streets and their bodies were shoved into the ducts of the elaborate water system, fouling it. The survivors scattered into the mountains to live in caves as their ancestors had, but building rooms with the curious key-shaped doors that had adorned their homes in the great city.

The sun lighted the top of the far canyon wall as we sat at the lip of the cave and sipped breakfast tea. It took little imagination to people the silent, domed chamber; to visualize men and women with high foreheads, wide cheekbones, large eyes and broad noses, their bodies short,

Remnants of mud walls and drainage ditches survive amid the ruins of Casas Grandes, site of a flourishing Indian city nearly 1,000 years ago.

lean and hard. One could almost see them mending the *trincheras* after a flood, or tending their small plots of corn, or striding with jugs on their heads carrying water from the spring.

But there was little time left for daydreams. If we were going to make our rendezvous with the truck we would have to leave. Instead of returning over the course we had taken up and down the legs of the centipede, Teodolo now led us directly up one side of its back and down the other side. The going was drier and hotter than on the previous afternoon, and I was soon tempted to break a reddish-purple fruit from one of the dozens of prickly-pear cacti that grew on the hillside. I knew it from a related variety I had bought in Puerto Rican markets in New York City.

What I did not know was that "prickly" hardly describes the vicious spines it is armed with in the wild. Gingerly holding one of the pears between thumb and forefinger, I peeled it with my knife. Before I was through my fingers were a mass of barbed needles, and while I gulped down the pulp I somehow managed to get more needles into my cheeks, lips and even into my tongue. Later I picked them out, painfully. But at the moment I hardly noticed them as I savored the glorious, sweet wetness of the fruit, a cross in taste and texture between a ripe peach and a Concord grape.

That succulent cactus was the first edible bounty that the Sierra yielded up to me, and I was grateful—even more so after Teodolo showed me, with some amusement, how the tuna, as it is called, is properly handled. He knocked some of the fruit off the ears of a cactus with a leafy oak twig and then rolled them around in the dirt until the spines were all broken off; the fruit could then be picked up and safely peeled and eaten. Teodolo also advised me to select nearly round fruit; the kind that was elongated and creased was less good. Round tuna were plentiful and I ate a dozen or more.

By noon we were back at the first ravine and began the long, punishing uphill climb that got us to the truck late that afternoon. Tiring as the intervening five hours were, my memory of that afternoon is totally overwhelmed by a single swift act to which I was sole and silent witness. Teodolo, despite the rheumatism of which he complained and the 71 years of which he was proud, was out of sight ahead of me up the trail. Dick was suffering from a case of blisters and had fallen behind. I was left all alone in the cooling shade of the tall forest canopy, following a mule track that twined back and forth across the shallow stream that flowed in the ravine.

An undertone of running water and the occasional chirp of a bird had been the only sounds I had heard for an hour when suddenly a raucous screech came from the slope just above. I looked up between the dappled trunks of lofty sycamores and saw a large hawk gliding down toward me through shafts of sunlight. It passed no more than 10 feet overhead. I had a vivid look at the source of the banshee screams: a black, white and red acorn woodpecker clutched in the hawk's strong talons, and still very much alive.

Just as the hawk swept near, the woods erupted with the cries of a dozen Mexican jays. They fluttered around the big bird scolding loudly as it flew by. The hawk alighted in the stream—to escape the pesky jays, I thought. But as the jays continued to dive at it, veering off at the last instant, the hawk paid them little heed. I realized then that it had another purpose. The high-pitched screeching of the woodpecker had stopped. The hawk was drowning it. Rather than administer the *coup de grâce* with its beak—and risk being pecked in the face by its thrashing victim—the hawk had taken this sophisticated method of finishing the job. A few minutes later it flew off downstream, clutching the now limp and silent woodpecker.

I have since asked half a dozen ornithologists if they have ever seen or heard of such a thing. None have. The Sierra Madre may have withheld from me its jaguars, its wolves and its grizzly bears. But at the 11th hour it had sent me that innovative hawk. Farther on I came to a sun-spattered pool, its bottom plastered with an intricate mosaic of leaves. Without a thought of halizone tablets, I lay on my stomach and drank deeply, easy at last in these maternal mountains.

Changing Face of the Desert

In most wild places, the changes that constantly take place on the earth's face are too slow to be perceptible —unless the landscape is violently rearranged by some natural cataclysm such as an earthquake or a volcanic eruption. But between the two great ranges of the Sierra Madre in the Chihuahuan Desert of northern Mexico, where the vegetation is too sparse either to conceal or seriously inhibit nature's abrasive forces, the consequences of weathering and erosion are so dramatically evident that they seem to be taking place before the eyes of the wilderness traveler. And indeed, in some ways they are. The desert floor is being steadily carpeted with materials from the mountaintops, washed or swept or blown down along slopes that are cracked and gullied by heat and water.

This area is part of a region geologists describe as being a basin-and-range province, which consists essentially of short mountain chains interspersed with broad, flat basins called bolsons (right). Unlike the extraordinarily well-watered bolson of Cuatro Ciénegas near the Sierra Madre Oriental (pages 68-83), these basins are dry for most of the year. Moreover their eroded materials have nowhere to go, for there are no river systems to carry them away. The few rivers that flow into the bolsons terminate in shallow lakes, which are really no more than huge puddles, gradually drying and filling under years of relentless sunshine.

The largest of these rivers, the Río Casas Grandes, originates high in the Sierra Madre Occidental. Here, rain clouds sweeping in from the west during the wetter summer months drop their moisture on the slopes; a number of rocky channels like the Arroyo de la Tinaja (pages 138-139) feed the water to the Casas Grandes. Collecting quantities of rock torn from the slopes by runoff, the river winds down onto the desert floor, leaving the coarser materials along the way and dumping the remaining muddy burden into Laguna de Guzmán (pages 140-141), the largest lake to be found in the area.

The materials transported down from the mountains—broken volcanic rocks such as quartz-bearing rhyolite and sedimentary rock such as limestone—become trapped in the lake bottoms and on the bolson floors. Thus, year by year, the bolsons are filling up, the lakes are becoming shallower, and the mountains are slowly melting away.

A small bolson, touched with new green growth that was stimulated by a recent rain shower, lies between two nameless mountains in the desert east of the Sierra Madre Occidental.

Rocky Channels Carved by Rains

For most of the year, the Arroyo de la Tinaja *(left)* and the rest of the eastern slopes of the Sierra Madre Occidental are bone dry. But in July, August and September as much as 17 inches of rain may fall, turning the arroyos into watery conduits for tens of thousands of tons of mountain debris.

While rain water booming through such gullies is the most powerful force in breaking down the mountains, other agents of destruction are also at work. Severe temperature changes flex and crack parts of the outer layers of the slopes. The roots of trees grow into crevices and muscle aside the rocky walls. Freezing water expands the fissures and causes chunks of rock to break off. Lichen growing on the rocks produce organic acids that assist in the disintegration of the surfaces.

Thus weakened, the mountains submit to the subsequent onslaught of rainstorms and runoff by giving up portions of their outer covering, like a snake shedding its skin. The rubble they yield continues to break down under the impact of pounding and tumbling as the water sweeps it into the arroyos and down toward the flats below.

Mists laden with moisture prepare to jettison their burden into the Arroyo de la Tinaja. The pink rock is mostly rhyolite, a volcanic material that will have been ground up into sand, silt and clay by the time it finishes its long journey to the desert flats.

Clawing at the earthen banks of the arroyo, runoff waters expose the roots of trees. At a point 14 miles farther downstream these waters will feed into the Río Casas Grandes, the ultimate transporter of the materials that have been eroded away from the area.

A River with No Place to Go

Fed by water from mountain arroyos, the Río Casas Grandes travels a lazy northward course until it reaches the desert. It then divides into a braiding of several channels, regathers and empties into Laguna de Guzmán, one of the few lakes in the region that contain water the year around. Although the river collects water from a drainage area of some 6,400 square miles and the lake also receives additional water both from rainfall and springs, the evaporation rate in this arid climate is so high that Laguna de Guzmán is never more than about three feet deep; usually it averages much less. The shallowness is all the more striking when compared to its other dimensions: length, about five miles; width, about two and a half miles.

Like all bolson lakes, this one has no outlets whatever. The sediments borne in by the river simply accumulate. Barring some major geological rearrangement of the area, Laguna de Guzmán will in time become filled with this debris. The lake will vanish, and in its place will be a dry, sandy plain.

The Río Casas Grandes (left) fans out nearly 500 feet as it approaches Laguna de Guzmán. Swollen by heavy rains, the river as shown in this photograph is some 40 times its usual width.

Mesquite trees stand trunk deep along the flooded fringe of Laguna de Guzmán (right) after 10 days of rain. These adaptable trees can withstand immersion for that long without dying.

The raised ridge of a fault line cuts across an immense dry plain below the Sierra de la Nariz. Materials carried off from this small range and others nearby make up the sedimentary fill on the basin floor. The fault line was created when the earth's outer crust split and the sediment on one side of the crack rose some 30 to 50 feet.

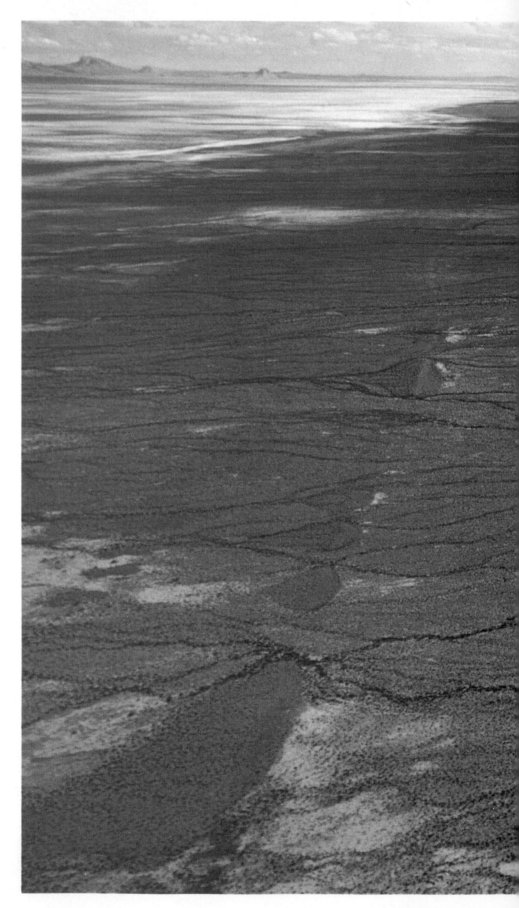

A summer cloudburst explodes over the bleak floor of the Bolsón de los Muertos—Basin of the Dead. Such downpours usually last no more than half an hour and occur only about 30 times a year. After a day or two, evaporation and absorption cause most or all of the water to disappear.

The Making of Sand Dunes

Most of the materials that come from the mountains into the bolsons do not rest exactly where they are first deposited; the elements combine in a variety of ways to carry them about. Wind-whipped waves along the margins of bolson lakes, for example, break down the sediment into ever smaller grains. During the long rainless season these minuscule particles lose their moisture, crumble apart and are ready to be moved.

In bolsons that happen to have no lakes, summer rainstorms turn the surfaces into quagmires, temporarily gluing the materials into a heavy clay. But the hot desert sun soon burns off the water, cracking the surface and releasing myriad particles to be borne away.

The westerlies that sweep this portion of the Chihuahuan Desert pick up the bits and pieces of rock from the dry bolson floors, further abrading and reducing their size and scattering them over the land. In most areas they are distributed randomly. But at one point near the eastern edge of the bolsons, two parallel ranges—the Sierra del Presidio and the Sierra de Samalayuca—form a trap where the grains of sand and other particles pile up in *medanos*, or dunes, up to 350 feet high. Many of the materials in these dunes have come a long way; some of the dominant quartz, for example, can be directly traced to the rock of the Sierra Madre Occidental—a distance of about 100 miles.

Long sieges of drought between storms leave a crazy-quilt pattern of cracks, some up to 10 feet wide, in the parched bolson floor.

Bathed in the soft light of sunset, sand dunes appear as cresting waves about to break upon the distant Sierra de Samalayuca. These

dunes, whose constantly drifting sands support little vegetation, are part of a field that covers an area of roughly 100 square miles.

5/ The Barranca Country

*At the sight of the precipice such was my
terror that I did not precisely dismount from
my mule, but let myself fall off on the side
opposite the precipice, sweating and trembling
all over with fright.* PADRE JUAN MARIA SALVATIERRA/ 1684

Throughout the long January night the conductor had called out all the stops. But this time, when the west-bound train of the Ferrocarril Chihuahua al Pacifico lurched to a halt, the only clue to our whereabouts was the hour. My watch showed just past six: the scheduled time of arrival at the whistle stop of Divisadero.

The moon had set and sunup was still to come. In the blackness beyond my window no sign of a station appeared. I dragged my backpack off the overhead rack and hurried up the aisle of the coach and onto the vestibule. Light and steam spilled into the frosty air. Wreathed in white billows, the conductor stood at the foot of the folded-down steps.

"Divisadero?" I shouted down.

"*Sí, señor!*"

No sooner was I standing on the crushed rock beside him than he began swinging his lantern, signaling to the head of the train. No other passenger had gotten off.

"Wait!" I yelled. "My dog—*mi perro!*" I began sprinting toward the baggage car up ahead. Just as I reached its gaping door the train began to move. "*Mi perro!*" I shouted wildly into the dim, cavernous space. The baggage man smacked his forehead and began pulling aside boxes that were piled in front of a small locker. Mournful howls were issuing from it. I was running now to keep up.

Patrick appeared. The rope leash with which I had entrusted him to the baggage man 10 hours earlier (along with a 20-peso tip) was still tied to his collar. The man leaned down and handed me the end of the rope. I pulled 35 pounds of uncertain hound out of the moving car and into my arms. Incredibly, at that very moment on the second set of rails at my back, a freight train rolled by in the opposite direction. Where I stood the tracks curved and the tortured couplings of the cars screamed maddeningly. I crouched between the trains, awash in noise, holding Patrick tightly, and getting my face licked.

Then the trains were past, and Patrick and I were left in silence, the pinpricks of stars the only light. I put him down; carefully, as much by feel as by sight, we made our way toward a dark shape near the tracks. It turned out to be a small wooden shed, securely padlocked. Reaching down to test the ground, my hand touched snow, the drifted remnants of a storm that had rendered the dirt road into this part of the sierra impassable, necessitating my trip by train. I found a clear spot and, keeping a firm grip on Patrick's rope, I hunkered down and waited. It would be at least an hour until sunrise and my first close look at the spectacle that had brought me to Divisadero: the immense gorges called barrancas.

Barranca. The very word, I thought, has the ring of grandeur. My dictionary had defined it merely as "a ravine, a gully, a canyon"; by that paltry definition barrancas are to be found anywhere in Mexico's mountains. But here on the western slope of the Sierra Madre Occidental I was about to encounter a barranca worthy of the name—a mammoth trench carved out by millions of years of erosion; a cut in the earth many miles long, several miles wide and in places almost as deep as that most celebrated of super trenches, the Grand Canyon of the United States. There are six such trenches in Mexico, all of them concentrated in an area loosely called the barranca country at the northern end of the Occidental range.

Flying low over the barranca country in a small plane some months earlier, I had tried to sort out its features. The peaks, rising as high as 8,000 feet, seemed from a distance to form an impenetrable wall; yet from directly overhead, the wall was spectacularly breached by canyons. Rivers seeking their way through the mountains toward the Gulf of California had cut through thousands of feet of volcanic rock, sometimes as far down as the primeval basement rock of the sierra. And centuries of torrential summer rains, sweeping eastward off the gulf, had helped to enlarge the gaps.

Each barranca had its own unique shape—or, more precisely, its complex of shapes. Those shapes included walls that plunged precipitously from the rim; other walls were buttressed by projecting ridges between which small arroyos sloped downward at relatively gentle inclines. The arroyos fed into larger, steeper-walled canyons below, which in turn swept down to the barranca bottoms. And there in each one, barely visible from on high, wound the river that, in some form or other, had started it all.

From Divisadero, where I now sat awaiting the sunrise, I had a choice of two adjacent barrancas to explore. Barranca del Cobre, or Copper Canyon—named for the mines that once probed into its flanks—was about two miles distant. Barranca de Urique lay directly in front of me —in fact, no more than a stone's throw, as I was to discover when daylight came. The same river, the Río Urique, had carved both gorges. I had formed a tentative plan, but I wanted to consult some local opinion before going ahead.

As night dissolved, I watched the panorama of the Barranca de Urique emerge like the image of a photograph in a developing tray. First came the general shapes of the crenelated cliff faces and the sharp profiles of ridges jutting from walls. Then came details: the rough grain of gray-green talus slopes, the black interior folds of arroyos. As the light increased, pine trees were outlined on slopes hundreds of feet below; they looked minute, though I judged they were not much smaller than the 60-foot specimens that surrounded me at the rim. I was surprised by the amount of vegetation I saw; I had expected much more exposure of bare rock.

The sun, now rising, had turned the rimrock of the barranca from a shadowy buff to a vivid pink. By this time, I was savoring the sight through the windows of a small, rustic hotel where I had taken refuge from the chill morning. As man-sized logs crackled in a stone fireplace, I outlined my plan to the hotel owner, Ingeniero Efrain Sandoval Loera, who had put up the building in 1972 right on the edge of the Barranca de Urique. What I wanted to do, I explained, was to descend to the river at the bottom of the barranca, using a trail I had heard led down from the rim near Divisadero. Then I proposed to follow the riverbed some 25 miles south to the tiny settlement of Urique, a former mining town nestled deep in the barranca. But back in Chihuahua I had been told that I could not get from Divisadero to Urique along the river; I would have to climb back up the same trail I went down, and take the railroad a few stops farther south to a place where another trail led down to the town of Urique. The way I figured it, that meant about a 5,000-foot climb down into the barranca, a 5,000-foot climb back out, and an equally arduous repeat down and up the second trail. Was all that really necessary?

"Not at all," said Sandoval. "You certainly can get to Urique along the river, and you can do it in three days." Had Sandoval ever made the trip himself? No. But, after all, he had known this country all his life; his father had owned land here before him. I would, of course, need the services of a guide—but Sandoval would find one for me. I was pleased and relieved.

At midday, my obliging host introduced me to Vicente Mancinas, a smiling Indian in his mid-20s, with the build of a skinny 12-year-old. He wore the tire-soled sandals that, winter and summer, are the universal footwear in this part of the sierra. All the while Sandoval talked to him he held his straw hat in his hand, revealing to us a head of close-cropped hair.

Could he take me to Urique by the river? Sandoval asked. Vicente's smile grew larger. "Sí, señor." We settled on a price—48 pesos a day (four dollars), equal to what he earned cutting timber for Sandoval; he collected a thin cotton blanket and a mesh bag which he filled with cooked tortillas and we set off together, with Patrick loping alongside.

Looking back now over the days that followed, I am struck by the contrast between the simple optimism of those first hours and the turbulence of wonder, surprise, fear and exhaustion that came later. The trail into the barranca lay about a mile west of Divisadero. To get there Vicente and I walked through a pleasant, snow-flecked forest of pine to a point where a small brook dipped over the barranca rim and down through a wide arroyo. As we followed the stream down, there was at first almost no sense of change; pine trees still surrounded us and the trail, a well-worn mule track, proved easy. But less than an hour later we emerged into the open, onto a wide, grassy, goat-cropped shoulder of the arroyo. The sky above was pure and cloudless. The sun radiated a dry warmth that was welcome after the remembered chill of my early morning arrival. The far side of the barranca, some six or seven miles away, filled the sky; its cliffs and talus slopes and grassy shoulders, much like the one we were on, formed a gigantic mosaic. Checking my pocket altimeter, I saw that we had descended about 1,500 feet from Divisadero; we had come more than a fourth of the way down to the river. Nothing to this barranca delving, I thought.

Three hours later, sprawled against a boulder in utter exhaustion, I felt considerably less confident. From the easy slope of the first arroyo we had descended into another, then down the steep side of a deep, V-shaped cleft that pointed directly toward the river. The careful placing of one foot in front of the other, the constant struggle to keep my balance under a 50-pound pack, had taken a toll. I had to call a halt. Patrick lay panting beside me. Vicente sat quietly on a rock, smoking a cigarette.

After a while I noticed that the ground under us, loose shale and powdery rock, was desert dry. The acacia and mesquite all around us, sprouting feathery new leaves, could thrive in this environment, but not a thirsty hiker. I drank the last of the water in my canteen and got to my feet; this was no place to pass the night. Vicente assured me that just a little farther down the canyon there was a spring; it even had a name, Aguas Calientes—Hot Waters. From there, he added encouragingly, it would be a matter of only a couple of hours more before we reached the river.

I shouldered my pack once again and we continued on down. The canyon walls pressed in closer, and I anxiously searched the narrowing slit of sky above us for signs of twilight. At one point, as I peered upward, I saw the yawning openings of several shallow caves that resembled the one I had visited at Guaynopa, on the eastern flank of the Occidental. I thought I heard dogs barking, and I asked Vicente if people lived in the caves. No, he said, I was hearing echoes. But again and again I heard the barking, along with the faint tinkle of cattle bells. Shepherd dogs, said Vicente, though I never did see them.

I heard Aguas Calientes before I saw it. The sound of running water in that dry gulch drew me quickly along the last 100 yards to where the stream gushed out of a jumble of boulders. Vicente soon had his shirt off and was washing it and himself in a shallow pool. I tried the water. It came from a thermal spring and was comfortably tepid. I lowered my bare tired body amid the rocks of a second shallow pool, and never had waters felt more restorative. Even so, I was too tired that night to cook supper. Instead I shared a can of tuna fish with Vicente. He began to brew some coffee, but before it was ready I was asleep.

When I awoke the next morning the first thing I saw was a grove of orange trees, planted all around the spring. That I had managed to overlook them the evening before could be attributed only to my fatigue. In any event, the sight of the grove struck me as a kind of miracle.

The jade-green Río Urique, placid in the winter low-water season, runs through the depths of the barranca it has carved.

Just 24 hours earlier, I had walked along the rim of the barranca with snow crunching beneath my feet. Since then we had descended far enough to reach a region where snow never falls.

The orange trees, the banana trees we later passed, the barking dogs, the tinkling cattle bells and the supposedly unoccupied caves I had spotted were all evidence of the shy, elusive people who winter on the lower slopes of the barrancas: the Tarahumara. Vicente was one of them, though by finding a job on the uplands he had abandoned the old way of life. I knew by now that there must be dozens, perhaps hundreds, of others living as they had done for generations along the route we would follow. As yet I had seen none but there was every chance that I would come across a hut or a herdsman tending his flock.

The Tarahumara live in thinly scattered family groups, moving back up into the higher reaches of the barrancas in May and June, when the time comes to harvest their wheat and plant beans and corn. All the Tarahumara, women as well as men, are extraordinarily agile climbers, maneuvering trails that would be impossible for an outsider like myself —even if I could find them.

Ironically, my own good Vicente chose this morning to lose his bearings. As we broke camp and continued on down the canyon, it suddenly occurred to me that Vicente had never walked the river from Divisadero to Urique. Our trail had vanished; as I watched my companion peering and probing, I realized that he was now serving more as a scout than as a guide.

The only choice we had was to stay close to the course of Aguas Calientes, but that became harder and harder to do. We were forced to climb over cabin-sized boulders and to inch our way along nearly vertical walls of sliding rock, hoping that the river would eventually come into view. Finally, after a couple of hours, we pushed through a thicket of reeds six feet tall and there it was, beyond a narrow sandy beach no more than about 30 yards long. Patrick, who was born at the seashore, went wild; the sight of sand ignited some dormant spark in him. He raced madly back and forth between the two rocky outcrops that marked either end of the beach. Then he spotted a stick and jammed on the brakes. Jackknifing, he grabbed the stick and tossed it into the air like a bull tossing a matador.

I, too, felt like running, out of a sheer sense of triumph. At last we had reached the river, about a mile below the first dip over the arroyo rim at Divisadero. From where we stood, everything was up, the obverse of standing on a mountaintop. Yet curiously, I experienced the same feeling of exultation that comes with scaling a high peak. The barranca's rock ribs were colored in greens, ochers and pale, earthy pinks. Where water spilled over cliffs or seeped out of crevices, the rock was stained in long black streaks. The river and its ancestral stream, which had achieved this prodigious work of excavation over a period of perhaps 10 million years, ran past us wide and shallow over a washboard of small rocks. In July, when the rains came, the Río Urique would turn into a charging fury, the air would be stifling, and the rocks would steam as though in a Turkish bath. Right now, however, the atmosphere was agreeably springlike, and both the barranca and the river were at their most benign.

Still, the trip along the river was not going to be easy; that became abundantly clear as I looked around. Several times, while sweating my way down a steep drop, I had comforted myself with the thought that once we reached bottom the going would be a ramble over more or less level terrain. That notion now vanished.

What I had not anticipated was the peculiarly serrated contours of the riverbanks—relatively short strips of beach separated by several hundred feet of sheer rock walls. The beaches were the beds of the canyons that bordered the river; the walls formed the ridges between adjoining canyons. Conceivably we could stick to one side of the river, but that would permit only the briefest progress along a stretch of beach before a rock wall blocked our way and had to be climbed; then there would be another small beach, then another wall to be scaled and descended, and so on for an indefinite distance.

There was only one way to get through this obstacle course. As we came to the end of a beach, we would have to ford the river, crossing and recrossing it to avail ourselves of whatever relatively level stretches we could find on either side. In short, the straightest route downstream was a zigzag.

As we prepared for our first fording, I looked enviously at Vicente's tire-soled sandals. Being amphibious, they were far more practical than my hiking boots for this work, but one must be born to those sandals to walk long distances in them. Fortunately, I had a pair of old sneakers in my backpack; they would at least partially protect my city-soft feet from the river rocks. As I sat and unlaced my boots, I could not foresee how many times I would be repeating this ritual, and perhaps that was just as well.

I had expected the Río Urique water to be considerably colder than

that at Aguas Calientes, but when I stepped in for the first time I was not prepared for the chill as the river covered my calves and soaked my rolled-up jeans. Unsteadily I teetered toward the far bank, bastioned with huge bleached-white boulders. The trunks of large trees were jammed between rocks 20 feet above water level, indicating the river's range and force when in flood.

When I reached the beach on the far side I stepped into a timeless world in which the only sign of man was the swaying bamboo-like reeds that grew profusely along the bank. These stout grasses were introduced into the New World by the Spanish colonizers. Otherwise this silent cove, sheltered by a deep crease in the earth, looked as I imagined it had for thousands of years.

There was something about this primeval place that made me want to stay. We had enough food to share for a week, there was no problem about water, and I would have welcomed the rest. But I stifled the impulse to suggest so startling a change of plan. This beach, too, ended in a wall of rock; we would have to cross the river again.

This time we had to strip because, as Vicente reported after reconnoitering, the ford was a lot deeper than the last one. Without clothes Vicente looked almost unbelievably emaciated; there was no fat on him and very little lean, and his legs were skeletal. Where he stored such reserves of energy on his meager frame I cannot imagine. He could not have weighed more than 90 pounds dripping wet, which was the way I shortly saw him. He had bundled his clothes and supplies in his blanket and slung it over his back. That proved to be a blunder. The water reached to his neck, and everything got soaked, including his much-prized cigarettes—later salvaged by a careful drying out on a rock in the sun.

My own river crossing was slightly less dampening because I had thought to hoist my backpack onto my head. I nearly dropped it as I stumbled over slippery, unseen rocks, but I had broken off a reed pole to balance myself. Patrick, following me, had his own problems; he was washed over a little waterfall into a pool. But he emerged none the worse for the surprise. Henceforth, when he had to swim, he waited first to see where Vicente reached the beach on the other side and then took care to start well upstream from that point.

I cannot remember how many times we crossed the river that day. In the evening we camped on a beach in a wide node of the canyon. Though the sky above us was still light, we were in deep shadow. The air felt

cold and I built a roaring fire with driftwood from a supply that lay near the river's high-water mark. Patrick wolfed down his daily ration of dried dog food, powdered milk and water, and flaked out on the sand. Vicente took a few cooked tortillas out of the stock with which he had started the trip and warmed them by laying them out on glowing coals raked from the fire. The tortillas and the coffee, heavily laced with sugar, comprised his basic fare. My own freeze-dried camping rations did not appeal to him, although he readily accepted all the dried fruit that I offered.

In the bustle of making camp, I hadn't even had a chance to survey our surroundings, but as we sat silently waiting for a pan of water to boil I swept my gaze across the far side of the canyon. To my surprise I picked out a small hut perched on the shoulder of a hill, with figures running about. Tarahumara Indians. Either they did not see us in our shadowed resting place, or they chose not to acknowledge it. In any case, eager to observe these people, so reticent when aware of strangers in their midst, I took out my field glasses and frankly spied on them. The figures turned out to be three children playing tag—two little girls dressed in ankle-length skirts and kerchiefs and a boy in short breeches. All three were barefoot. I had heard that the Tarahumara can run deer and turkeys to exhaustion; I had also been told of a game they play, in which two teams race for as long as 48 hours without rest while kicking a wooden ball. This legendary stamina is evidently developed from early childhood.

The hut was built on a narrow shelf of terraced land, and smoke rose from its chimney. From the precipitous slope above, a young woman and a dog were bringing down a herd of goats. Night was falling, but the woman appeared to be in no hurry. No doubt it would have been dangerous to rush the animals. The scene was something straight out of *Heidi,* with the exception that scrappy patches of cactus and mesquite took the place of Alpine meadowland.

The Tarahumara live primitively in the barrancas, more closely in touch with the land than most of the other scant remnants of North American aborigines. They keep goats and cattle, yet they rarely eat them. The livestock is used chiefly to supply manure; the barrancas are too steep in most places to accumulate much topsoil. The herd the young woman was bringing down the mountainside that evening was probably penned up later in a cave or stone corral from which manure could be gathered for the corn and bean fields. On slightly more level

This Lumholtz photograph shows a Tarahumara family in the shallow cave they used as a winter shelter at the bottom of a barranca.

land an enclosure might be made of log rails, then dismantled and moved around a fallow field every few days. Thus the Tarahumara lead lives midway between settled farmers and nomadic herdsmen.

Sometime in the middle of the night I awakened; I opened my eyes to see the light of a full moon spilling through the barranca walls. As I watched, clouds scudded past, turning the sky darkly luminous. Could it mean rain?

The next morning, as I sat sipping a cup of tea, a young Tarahumara man appeared across the wide, riffling river, walking downstream along a beach we had followed the day before. For us it had ended at a sheer wall of rock, and we had gone back up the beach to a shallow ford, then crossed to the place where we camped. As I watched, the man continued straight at the rock face without breaking stride. He then moved across it as easily as a fly walks across a wall. He never once used his hands, relying completely on footholds; very likely he walked that way every morning. Disappearing through a cleft, he reappeared farther down river only a few minutes later, still walking at an easy pace. I felt a twinge of inadequacy; covering approximately the same distance by zigzagging across the river had taken us at least half an hour. Señor Sandoval had no doubt been right. Someone could make Urique in three days from Divisadero, but obviously I was not that someone.

Later that morning we forded the river for the umpteenth time. The crossing looked routine—first rocks and gravel, then a long sandbar that led to a beach on the other bank—so I elected to go first. But when I stepped onto the bar I suddenly sank into it up to my thigh. Quicksand. The first sickening drop produced an adrenaline charge that nearly made me faint. I was hip deep and fumbling with my waist strap to get out of my backpack when I stopped sinking. By leaning forward and bending my knees I found that I could sort of crawl up onto the surface of the sand and drag myself onto more solid footing. Previously I had observed Vicente probe at similar sandbars with his reed pole. Now I knew why.

Then it began to rain. We found shelter beneath a house-sized boulder on the beach and sprawled there for nearly an hour waiting for the rain to stop. Little rivulets of water, defying gravity, clung to the concave rock face that framed our view downstream, then dropped with a splat at our feet. The opposite bank was backed by a 60-foot cliff, its surface covered with rocky rubble amid which grew agave, acacia and organ cactus. There were several large trees with thumb-sized blunt knobs scattered over elephant-gray trunks—wild kapok trees with their milkweed-like pods still tightly shut. In the late winter the pods would burst open, releasing their seed-bearing cottony tufts to be carried off by the wind.

Then I noticed another tree, leafless but covered with large white trumpet-shaped blossoms that have given it the name morning-glory tree; Vicente called it palo blanco. The tree had already shed its leaves in anticipation of the barranca dry season, which would soon begin. Without leaves palo blanco would be able to conserve water better; then, when the rainy season began toward the end of June, it would scatter its seed. Triggered by the rains, other flowering trees would festoon the barrancas with gaudy blooms—the rich yellow flowers of the red stick tree, the tiny rose-colored balls of the albizia tree. And acacia blossoms would fill the night with their sweet scent.

I was too early for the annual greening of the barrancas, but the massive forms I saw gleaming that afternoon through the gray veil of pelting rain were a sight for all seasons. Downstream, above and beyond the tree-studded cliff, the canyon opened out into a grandiose and wildly romantic scene that would have enraptured a 19th Century landscape artist. A triangular mass of rock rose 1,000 feet from the riverbed like a Maya pyramid. This towering monument had been left behind as the jut of highland between two adjoining arroyos that had gradually eroded away. Now only this pinnacle remained, and behind it a backdrop of angular rock faces receded into the clouds.

When the rain stopped we moved on. Gradually the character of the barranca changed. Massive boulders choked the river, separating its waters into strong, white, arching sinews. We spent most of the rest of the afternoon clambering up, over, around and sometimes under these enormous stones. Finally we could go no farther. Ahead, the river ran between two parallel walls of rock. Our route, if it was a route, went straight up a cliff. For a Tarahumara it presented no problem. For me, with Patrick and the pack, it was impossible. I suggested that we stop for the night.

Early the next morning I stood beside the river shivering. All I had on were my sneakers and, on a lanyard around my neck, my Swiss Army knife and the key to my car back in Chihuahua. Everything else was wrapped inside a huge bundle balanced on my head. All critical items—camera, binoculars, and food—were stowed in Ziplock plastic bags. My poncho served as the outer layer of the bundle. My hope was that with the pack's aluminum frame to prevent it from collapsing, the bundle would float, at least long enough to get me some 200 yards down river, where it appeared I could clamber out onto a narrow gravel bank.

Luckily, the bundle did not have to pass the flotation test. As I waded into the piercingly cold water I found a hard-packed sandbar that ran down the center of the riverbed. Carefully probing with my reed pole, I followed it the whole way, with the water never getting deeper than my chin. Patrick swam easily by my side. Vicente decided he would prefer climbing the near-vertical cliff. He managed to do so in such short order that I was still drying myself when he joined me on the gravel bank.

As we moved along, the walls of the barranca trench became more and more precipitous. We found fewer and fewer places to walk at the river's edge. Instead we had to maneuver steep trails, often only half a foot wide, some 50 to 100 feet above river level; they were really no more than shallow grooves in the flanks of the barranca. The footing was crumbly shale, given to sliding out from under a boot and tumbling downward—a constant reminder of our own precarious situation. There was virtually nothing to hold on to. But Vicente paced these trails as if he were on a Sunday stroll, and even Patrick ran ahead, quite oblivious to any danger. I took each step with the utmost caution, using my reed pole to steady my balance, wholly preoccupied with finding a safe foothold. Only once was I distracted, when on one ledge we came to a kind of pothole, not much bigger than a bathtub, with a rim of rocks cemented around it. According to Vicente, it had once been used by gold prospectors to wash ore. When? Oh, long, long ago.

Near the day's end we were able to descend once more to the river's edge. Upstream at many points the Río Urique had been as much as 60 yards wide; here it flowed between towering rock jaws no more than 50 feet apart. Large clots of dried grass and jumbles of twigs were caught in the tops of the scrubby acacia and mesquite trees along the walls—debris accumulated when the Río Urique was in spate during the summer and tried to squeeze through the narrow gorge. The dark rock at the entrance to the gorge had been polished to a metallic sheen by the repeated rush of water. We set up camp on a patch of beach so small it barely held us all. But during the night this choice of a campsite seemed eminently worthwhile. I awoke several times profoundly convinced that I could hear whistling and singing. The scientific explanation would have been that the smooth, narrow rock walls were sifting out a few high overtones from the surging noise of the river.

On the last day of his adventure in the barrancas of the Sierra Madre, author Peter Wood's dog Patrick raises his nose to yet one more fresh smell at a campsite along the Río Urique.

This was possible; but I favored my own private theory—water sprites.

The next morning I could still hear the river singing, though I was now 1,000 feet above the gorge. The climb, following the only trail we could detect, had been strenuous, but our reward from this vantage was a magnificent view of the way we had come.

There was also something less cheering: a view of the way we still had to go. To the south the river ran in a series of shallow S curves along a single compass bearing for many miles. With that to go on, I was able for the first time to pinpoint our location on my map. Three days on the river had brought us barely 15 miles from Divisadero. It was nearly as far again to the town of Urique.

All that day we could make progress down river only by following trails that hugged the barranca's walls. The day was dull and sunless; my watch had stopped running and I lost all track of time until I saw flitting bats—a sure sign that dusk was near. An unexpected stroke of luck was nigh, too; we found a trail that led down to the river again, to a snug beach above a green pool of water. In it a single red-headed duck was paddling; at our arrival it quickly flew off. A large fig tree overhung the beach, its roots gripping the cliff face immediately above like gray serpents. Sometimes these trees sprout on the barranca walls and send their roots down as much as 30 to 40 feet in order to reach water; this tree was low enough so that I could hang my gear on its branches. It was an idyllic site—and, as it turned out, our last camp on the river.

The next morning found Patrick and me cowering under the poncho I had rigged in the fig tree. All throughout the night it had rained. Everything was soaked, including my down sleeping bag. Vicente was nowhere to be seen; he had discovered a cave somewhere nearby and had taken shelter inside it. I stirred the previous night's campfire and, huddling beside it, made a grim decision: we would give up our attempt to reach Urique.

I was determined, however, not to go back the way we had come. We would press ahead and climb out as soon as we found an opportunity. Once we had emerged atop the barranca's rim, we would be in the sierra highland—relatively level country where we would find established trails to cover the 30-odd miles out to a main road where we could hitch a ride back to civilization.

When Vicente reappeared, I told him my plan. He listened impassively, although I thought I detected a faint smile on his face. I quickly gathered up my gear, squeezing my wet sleeping bag into my backpack, and we set off. About a mile down river the Río Urique began to veer sharply to the west, and simultaneously our passage to the east appeared: the narrow opening of an arroyo that funneled a tributary, the Río Hondo, into the barranca channel. About a quarter of a mile farther up the arroyo the stream forked. The right fork, according to my map, headed in the direction of Cieneguita, a little lumbering town in the highlands. We took this fork and almost immediately the banks of the stream closed in steeply, giving us little or no walking room. Before long I was sopping wet, both from the stream and from the damp, waist-high grass that bordered it. No animals had grazed in this area for a long time and there was no trail at all. We simply kept following the stream, hoping for the best.

Then something unexpected came into view. Up ahead of us the stream turned into a ribbon of white spilling down over a cliff several hundred feet high. We could either retrace our steps or search for a trail up the cliff.

An hour or so later we were scrambling upward through dense jungly undergrowth, dripping ferns, high grasses, vines and *mala mujer.* This was the only time during the entire trip that I found an occasion to use the machete that I had bought impulsively when I started out, never had sharpened, and simply carried strapped to my backpack all that time in the barranca. In front of us a wet and slimy 30-foot rock face rose up; scaling that obstacle would be the first test of our ability to get over the cliff.

The ascent was grueling. After the first 30 feet, in which we took turns boosting each other, the backpack and Patrick from ledge to ledge, there were another 200 or 300 feet of near-vertical climb. We were able to negotiate it only because of the small shrubs and trees, barely nourished by their topsoil, which provided us with handholds. Often we used a long, tough reed pole as a sort of life line, hauling each other up with it.

When at last we reached the summit of the cliff we could see the top of the waterfall spurting over a ledge some feet below us. I felt jubilant. In my exit from the barranca I had scaled a precipice so dizzying it made everything I had done before seem tame.

Vicente, too, recognized the ascent as an accomplishment. At the top of the cliff was a knife-edged ridge; following its contours would lead us southeast to the town of Cieneguita. But before we went on, Vicente walked to a place where the ridge overhung the cliff. With nothing but space around him on three sides he stood looking out for a few min-

Author Peter Wood recorded the last moment of his Sierra Madre trek with this photograph of his Tarahumara Indian guide, Vicente Mancinas. Behind Vicente is the craggy corridor that led the two out of the barranca country. In the left foreground is the author's baggage, his staff and the machete he carried and used only once.

utes, quietly yet triumphantly. I called to him and indicated that I wanted to take his picture. He pushed his hat back on his head and turned a serious Indian face to the camera. I snapped the picture, and we turned toward Cieneguita.

Weeks later, seated on a soft sofa in a Manhattan apartment, I stared long and wistfully at that picture. Technically it was imperfect, the light dull, the exposure not quite right. My open camera bag sat in the foreground. There too, as if to mock me, lay the nearly superfluous machete, carried up the slope by Vicente and later, at Cieneguita, politely refused by him when I offered it as a parting gift. (Back in New York it had at last found service as a souvenir.)

Now, as I take the picture out from time to time to look at it, the symbolism remains better than the technique. Everywhere there are rocks, the stuff the Sierra Madre is made of. And in the low-hanging clouds there is a hint of water, the soft, insistent element that has fractured and hewed this country into so formidable a shape. In the middle of it all, very small yet quite undaunted, is the face of the Tarahumara, Vicente. Outside the frame, but very much part of the picture am I, holding the camera: 20th Century urban man, come to claim from the barrancas my own small share of the ultimate treasure of the Sierra Madre—its wild, awesome beauty.

In the years ahead thousands of similar photographs will probably find their way back to high-rise apartments. Even now, new roads are being built into the area and tourists in air-conditioned cars may some day enter the barrancas and pose on the edge of other cliffs against equally impressive backdrops. I hope not. And I know that only those who have walked there and slept there and grown weary and sometimes frightened by the depths and the heights will have known the real power, as well as the glory, of the Sierra Madre.

Austere Beauty of a Far Place

Within the Sierra Madre, photographer Dan Budnik sought out a place that would epitomize in pictures the range's special qualities—the sere landscape; the forbidding walls of rock; the sense of remoteness; and the surprising life forms that exist in a harsh climate. After consulting with geologists and botanists, Budnik picked the Barranca Sinforosa, a deep canyon on the Río Verde in the northern Sierra Madre Occidental.

The choice could not have been more apt, as he soon learned. His trip to the barranca took him progressively backward in time. He traveled by jet to the city of Chihuahua, by train to the frontier town of Creel, by lumber truck and dilapidated World War II Jeep to the barranca's edge, and then by mule and by foot into the barranca itself.

When he first approached the barranca, says Budnik, its appearance was deceptive; tall pine trees cast a cool shade, and the trail at that point ran by a stretch of lush, inviting shrubbery. But the seven-hour descent, an arduous climb down precipitous walls of volcanic rock along a little-used path, led him into the real world of the Sierra. It was April, the height of the dry season. Unfed by rain for two months, the river was at its lowest—only a few feet deep at some points—exposing 15-foot-high boulders *(page 173).*

Budnik spent six days and nights in the canyon, sleeping in a tent on the dried riverbed with the tent flap tightly zipped against evening sandstorms. His diet was a combination of freeze-dried food and prickly-pear cactus with the spines shaved off. Every day he got up with the sun and roamed the barranca, learning its topography, adjusting to its austerity, focusing on details that he had overlooked in his first sweeping glances. As he searched he discovered a wealth of contrasts: heat and cold, darkness and light, water and dust. Within the canyon's rocky embrace he also found a variety of life and color—a delicate orchid, the roots of a wild-fig tree, a tenacious cactus, a tiny hummingbird sipping nectar from the brilliant-red blossom of a chilicote tree.

In all he discovered the barranca to be an intensely appealing place, for which he developed a feeling not only of intimacy but also of increasing affection as the days went by. And when he left, it was with an awareness of a fresh kind of beauty that he had never expected to find in this far realm.

A SHAFT OF MORNING SUN ON LEDGE-TOP TREES

A VIOLET-CROWNED HUMMINGBIRD ABOUT TO FEED FROM CHILICOTE BLOSSOMS

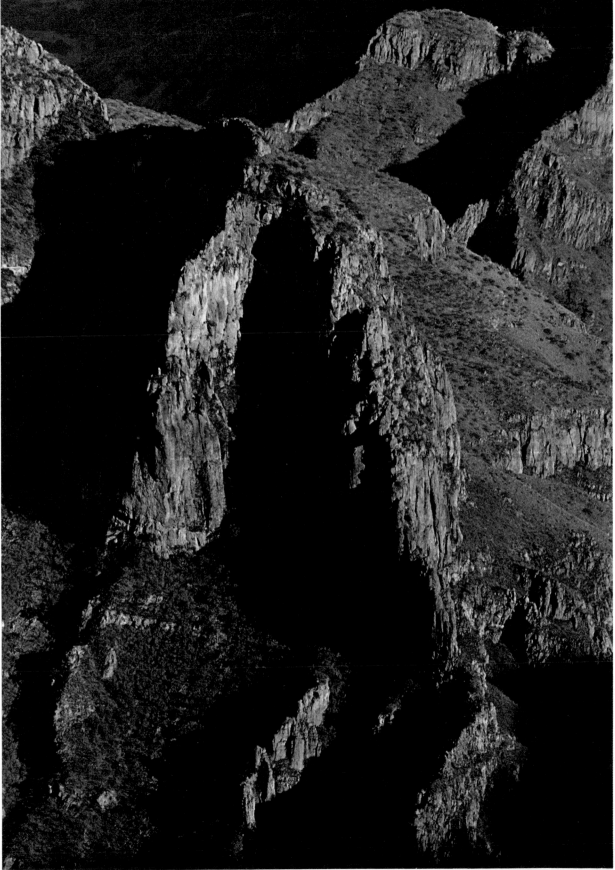

RAGGED RIDGES AT THE BARRANCA RIM

A CACTUS GARDEN CLINGING TO A CLIFF FACE

TANGLED BRANCHES OF A COPAL TREE

BOULDERS OF VOLCANIC ROCK IN THE RIVERBED

SAW-TOOTHED AGAVE LEAVES ON THE BARRANCA CREST

LADIES'-TRESSES BLOSSOMS BRUSHING A CHILICOTE BRANCH

A MASSIVE CAMUCHIN FIG ROOT SCARRED BY WATERBORNE DEBRIS

SINUOUS ROOTS OF A TESCALAMA FIG

A SUN-BATHED BARRANCA WALL AT MOONSET

Bibliography

*Also available in paperback.
†Available only in paperback.

†Alden, Peter, Finding the Birds in Western Mexico. University of Arizona Press, 1969.

Blake, Emmet Reid, Birds of Mexico: A Guide for Field Identification. University of Chicago Press, 1953.

Comstock, John Henry, The Spider Book. Cornell University Press, 1971.

Correll, Donovan Stewart, Native Orchids of North America North of Mexico. Chronica Botanica Company, Waltham, Massachusetts, 1950.

Correll, Donovan Stewart and Marshall Conring Johnston, Manual of the Vascular Plants of Texas. Texas Research Foundation, 1970.

Crow, John A., Mexico Today. Harper and Brothers, 1957.

*Davis, L. Irby, A Field Guide to the Birds of Mexico and Central America. University of Texas Press, 1972.

De Vaca, Cabeza, Adventures in the Unknown Interior of America. Cyclone Covey, ed. and trans. Collier Books, 1961.

Díaz del Castillo, Bernal, The Discovery and Conquest of Mexico. Farrar, Straus and Cudahy, 1956.

†Edwards, Ernest P., A Field Guide to the Birds of Mexico. Ernest P. Edwards, Sweet Briar, Virginia, 1972.

Hawkes, Alex D., Encyclopedia of Cultivated Orchids. Faber and Faber Limited, London, 1965.

*Horgan, Paul, Great River: The Rio Grande in North American History, 2 vols. Rinehart and Company, 1954.

Jenkinson, Michael, Wild Rivers of North America. E. P. Dutton and Company, 1973.

Leopold, A. Starker, Wildlife of Mexico. University of California Press, 1959.

Lister, Florence C. and Robert H., Chihuahua: Storehouse of Storms. University of New Mexico Press, 1966.

Lumholtz, Carl, Unknown Mexico, 2 vols. Charles Scribner's Sons, 1902.

Madison, Virginia, The Big Bend Country of Texas. October House, New York, 1955.

†Maxwell, Ross A., The Big Bend of the Rio Grande. Guidebook 7, University of Texas Press, 1971.

Mohr, Charles E. and Thomas L. Poulson, The Life of the Cave. McGraw-Hill Book Company, 1966.

Pennington, Campbell W., The Tarahumar of Mexico: Their Environment and Material Culture. University of Utah Press, 1963.

Pesman, M. Walter, Meet Flora Mexicana. Dale Stuart King, Globe, Arizona, 1962.

Peterson, Roger Tory, and Edward L. Chalif, A Field Guide to Mexican Birds. Houghton Mifflin Company, 1973.

Peterson, Russell, Silently, By Night. McGraw-Hill Book Company, 1964.

†Scott, W. Ray, Big Bend National Park. National Park Concessions, 1961.

Slaughter, Bob H., and Dan W. Walton, About Bats. Southern Methodist University Press, 1970.

Smith, C. Henry, The Story of the Mennonites. Mennonite Publication Office, 1950.

Standley, Paul C., Trees and Shrubs of Mexico. Vol. 23, Parts 1-3 of Contributions from the U.S. National Herbarium. Smithsonian Institution, 1920-1926.

Tamayo, Jorge L., Geografía General de México. Pub. Mexico, 1949.

Thrapp, Dan L., The Conquest of Apacheria. University of Oklahoma Press, 1967.

Vines, Robert A., Trees, Shrubs and Woody Vines of the Southwest. University of Texas Press, 1960.

Wallace, Ernest and E. Adamson Hoebel, Comanches, Lords of the South Plains. University of Oklahoma Press, 1952.

West, Robert C., ed., Handbook of Middle American Indians, Vol. 1. University of Texas Press, 1960.

West, Robert C., and John P. Augelli, Middle America: Its Lands and Peoples. Prentice-Hall, 1966.

Whetten, Nathan L., Rural Mexico. University of Chicago Press, 1948.

Williams, L. O., The Orchidaceae of Mexico. Escuela Agrícola Panamericana, Honduras, 1965.

Periodicals and Bulletins:

Dressler, Robert L., "Tropical Orchids near the Texas Border." American Orchid Society Bulletin, December 1961.

Hernandez, Crum, Fox, and Sharp, "A Unique Vegetational Area in Tamaulipas." Bulletin of the Torrey Botanical Club, November 1951.

Leopold, A. Starker, "Vegetation Zones of Mexico." Ecology, Vol. 31, No. 4.

Martin, Paul S., "A Biogeography of Reptiles and Amphibians in the Gómez Farías Region, Tamaulipas, Mexico. ' Miscellaneous Publications, Museum of Zoology, University of Michigan, April 15, 1958.

Martin, Paul S., "Zonal Distribution of Vertebrates in a Mexican Cloud Forest." The American Naturalist, Vol. 89, No. 849, November-December 1955.

Minckley, W. L., Environments of the Bolsón of Cuatro Ciénegas, Coahuila, México. Science Series No. 2, Texas Western Press, 1969.

Safford, William Edwin, "Sacred Flowers of the Aztecs." Volta Review, Vol. 14, No. 2, May 1912.

Schmidt, Robert H., Jr., A Geographical Survey of Chihuahua. Monograph No. 37, Texas Western Press, 1973.

Taylor, D. W. and W. L. Minckley, "New World for Biologist." Pacific Discovery, September-October 1966.

Williams, Stanley C., "Scorpions from Northern Mexico: Five New Species of Vejovis from Coahuila, Mexico." Occasional Papers of the California Academy of Sciences No. 68, September 25, 1968.

Acknowledgments

The authors and editors of this book are particularly indebted to the following people. In Arizona: W. L. Minckley, Associate Professor, Department of Zoology, Arizona State University, Tempe; Paul S. Martin, Professor of Geosciences, University of Arizona, Tucson. In Texas: George Burdick, Big Bend National Park; Dwight Deal, General Manager, Chihuahuan Desert Research Institute, Alpine; Barbara Warburton, Chairman, and Rodney Sullivan, Natural Science Department, Texas Southmost College, Brownsville; Stephen Clabaugh, Professor of Geology, Marshall C. Johnston, Professor of Botany, Robert H. Schmidt Jr., Associate Professor of Geological Sciences (El Paso), and Tom Wendt, Department of Botany, University of Texas, Austin; Dr. John Baker, Dallas; Ronald G. Fiesler and Fred S. Webster Jr., Austin. Also, Peter Alden, Natural History Tour Director, Massachusetts Audubon Society, Cambridge; Robert Bye Jr., Research Assistant, Botanical Museum, Harvard University, Cambridge; Ernest P. Edwards, Professor of Biology, Sweet Briar College, Sweet Briar, Virginia; Aaron J. Sharp, Distinguished Service Professor Emeritus, University of Tennessee, Knoxville. They also wish to thank the following persons and institutions. In Arizona: Charles C. DiPeso, Amerind Foundation, Dragoon; Donald J. Pinkava, Associate Professor of Botany, Arizona State University; Lyle K. Sowls, Professor, Wildlife Research Unit, University of Arizona. In Mexico: Ruperto y Esperansa Amador, Ramiro Flores Arizpe, Manuel Enriquez Barbier, Leonel Esquivel, Angel Riusech Fabrigat, Teodolo Yanez Gandara, Vicente Mancinas, José-Louis Rojas, Efrain Sandoval Loera, Manuel de los Santos and Sergio Veruete, Chihuahua; Diederich Friesen, Cuauhtemoc; Allan R. Phillips, San Nicolas de los Garza; Padre Carlos Zeyen, Cuatro Ciénegas de Carranza. In Mexico City: Arturo Gomez-Pompa, Professor, Departamento de Botanica, Instituto de Biologia; Enriqueta Garcia Miranda; Jerry Rzedowski, Professor, Escuela Nacional de Sciencia y Biologia and Bernardo Villa-Ramirez. In New York City: Robert Arbib, National Audubon Society; Donald Bruning, Associate Curator of Ornithology, Bronx Zoological Park; Arlene Holden, American Geographical Society; Sidney S. Horenstein, Department of Invertebrate Paleontology, The American Museum of Natural History; Larry G. Pardue, Plant Information Specialist, New York Botanical Garden. In Texas: Bob Burleson, Temple; Walter Dalquest, Professor of Biology, Midwestern State University, Wichita Falls; Victor Emmanuel, Houston; Jeremiah Epstein, Professor of Anthropology, Robert Harms, Chairman, Department of Linguistics, and Wann Langston, Professor of Geology, University of Texas, Austin; Campbell W. Pennington, Professor and Head of Department of Geography, Texas A & M, College Station; Richard Phelan, McGregor; William Rabenstein, Chief Park Naturalist, Big Bend National Park; James Reddell, Biology Department, and Ernest Wallace, Professor of History, Texas Tech University, Lubbock; David Riskind, Texas Parks and Wildlife Department, Austin. Others: Harry Clench, Associate Curator, Section of Insects and Spiders and C. J. McCoy, Curator, Section of Amphibians and Reptiles, Carnegie Museum of Natural History, Pittsburgh; George C. Eickwort, Associate Professor of Entomology, and Catherine A. Tauber, Research Associate, Department of Entomology, Cornell University, Ithaca, New York; Alan Graham, Professor of Botany, Kent State University, Kent, Ohio; Paul Krausman, College of Forestry, University of Idaho, Moscow; Douglas Lawson, Department of Paleontology, University of California, Berkeley; John M. Legler, Professor of Biology, University of Utah, Salt Lake City; R. H. Lister, National Park Service, Albuquerque, New Mexico; Rogers McVaugh, Director of Herbarium, University of Michigan, Ann Arbor; Charles A. Munn III, Owings Mills, Maryland; Ben Tinker, Rialto, California; Roland Wauer, National Park Service, Santa Fe, New Mexico; Louis O. Williams, Curator Emeritus, Field Museum of National History, Chicago.

Picture Credits

Index

*Numerals in italics indicate a
photograph or drawing of the subject
mentioned.*

A

Acacia(s), 82, 106, 128, 130, 152, 160;
flowers, 161
Agave(s), 81, 128, 160 *(Agave
americana), 174;* century plants, 32,
34; lechuguilla *(Agave lecheguilla),
26, 54, 80, 81, 82;* **spiny** *(Agave
lopantha), 116-117*
Agriculture, Mexican: candelilla, 26;
cane, 85; coffee, 22, 61, 62; oranges,
153-154
Alsate (Indian chief), 29
Animals: biotic province of Sierra
Madre, 21; jungle, 22; poisonous,
32, 70; protected species, 87;
watering holes, 36. *See also* specific
types
Antlion(s), *71*
Arbib, Robert, 91, 100
Arroyo(s): Occidental, 16, 150; Cuatro
Ciénegas, *2-3*
Arroyo de Guaynopa, 125, 126, *128-129,*
130
Arroyo de la Tinaja, 136, *138-139*
Arthrostemma flower(s)
(Arthrostemma ciliatum), 115

B

Banana tree(s), 61, 154
Barranca(s), 16, 22, 28, 118, 149, *158-159,*
160
Barranca del Cobre, *cover, 7,* 16, 150
Barranca Sinforosa, *166-167, 169, 178-
179*
Barranca de Urique: hike through, 150-
165; Indian inhabitants, 154, 158-160,
161
Basaseáchic Falls, *6-7,* 22
Bat(s), vampire, 59-60
Beetle(s), blister, *71*
Beverly, Jarvis, 92, 94, 96
Big Bend National Park (Texas), 20-21,

23, 24-35, 36; area, 20, 24; early
explorers, 29, 31; geological history,
27-29; life forms, 24-27
Bignonia(s), *106*
Bird(s): and birdwatching, 88-89, 91-
103; of cloud forest, 84; endangered
species, 96, 126; hunters, 87, 99;
migratory, 87-88, *96-97,* 99; rare
sightings, 102-103. *See also* specific
types
Bolla(s), copperhead *(Bolla
cupreiceps), 89*
Bolsón(s), 68, *136-137,* 144, *145;* lakes,
140
Bolsón de los Muertos, *144*
Bromeliad(s), *106*
Budnik, Dan, 68, 166
Bulrush(es) *(Scirpus olneyi), 78-79*
Burdick, George, 32-35
Butterflies, 61, *89,* 121

C

Cacti, 128, 158, 166, *170-171;* blind
prickly pear *(Opuntia rufida),* 26, *82-
83;* desert Christmas *(Opuntia
leptocaulis), 69;* garambullo
(Myrtillocactus geometrizans), 8-9;
hedgehog, 26; hikuli *(Lophophora
williamsii), 156;* organ, 160; pitahaya,
34-35; prickly pear, 32, 34, *40-41, 50-
51,* 54, 106, 134, 166; Rhipsalis
(Rhipsalis cassutha), 113
Calico butterfly *(Hamadryas februa),
89*
Caltrop *(Kallstroemia grandiflora),*
orange, *12-13*
Candelilla *(Euphorbia antisyphilitica),
24-25,* 26
Casas Grandes, *132-133*
Cave(s): as dwellings, *158-159;* life
forms, 59; limestone formations, 54,
55, *56,* 57; Occidental range, 126, 127,
128-129, 131, 132, 152; Oriental range,
16, 22, 52-60
Chalif, Edward L., 92
Chihuahua, 96, 118, 119, 126, 166
Chihuahuan Desert, *4-5,* 21, *136-147*
Chilicote tree(s) *(Erythrina
flabelliformis),* 166, *168, 175*
Chisos Basin, 33
Chisos Mountains, *22-23,* 24, 26, *30;*

fossils, 28; geology, 31-32; life forms,
31-35
Cichlid(s), 78, *79*
Clay, 93, 139, 144
Clorinde *(Anteos clorinde nivifera), 89*
Conservation: of caves, 56-57, 62; of
cloud forest, 90; endangered species,
87, 96, 126; preserves and refuges, 20,
21, 104; and tourism, 20, 165; water
control, 36, 41
Copal tree(s), *172*
Cortés, Hernando, *86,* 87
Cougar(s), 31-32, 34, 54, 85
Creosote bush(es), 22, 54, 80
Croton shrub(s) *(Croton ciliato-
glandulosus), 106*
Cuatro Ciénegas, *2-3;* geology, 68, 70,
73, 81-82; life forms, 69-83
Cypress(es), 33, 106; Montezuma bald
(Taxodium mucronatum), 107

D

Dahlia(s), 108; *(Dahlia coccinea), 114*
Damselflies, *78*
Davis, Irby, 91
Deal, Dwight, 28-29, 52, 53, 58, 60, 61,
62, 65-66
Deer, white-tailed, 31, 120
Desert(s), 22, 27, 36
Díaz del Castillo, Bernal, 87; quoted, 84
Duck(s): pintail, 96, 99; red-headed, 163
Dune(s): gypsum, 68, *70;* sand, *4-5,* 144,
146-147
Dyssodia gypsophilia, 68, *69*

E

Edwards, Ernest P., 91
Ericameria, 68-69
Erosion: alluvial slope, *80;* barranca
formation, 16, 149; of limestone, 16,
47, 54, 66; of mountains, 21, 136;
pothole formation, 41; rainwater, 139;
sedimentary fill, 142
Esperanza, 36, *48-49*
Euphonia, blue-hooded *(Euphonia
elegantissima), 95,* 103

F

Fig tree(s), 106, 163, 166; camuchin
(Ficus pertusa), 176; tescalma *(Ficus
petiolaris), 177*

Flycatcher(s), 87; vermilion
(*Pyrocephalus rubinus*), *94-95*
Forest(s), *10-11*; cloud, 84, 104, *108-109*,
111; logging, 122, 126, 127; pine, 22,
54, 93; tropical deciduous, 88, 104, 106

G

Geese, 87; lesser snow (*Anser
caerulescens hyperborea*), *96-97*;
snow, 99; white-fronted, 99
Geology: basin-and-range province,
136; faulting, 28, 66, *142-143*; flood
plains, 20, 28; karst, 54-55, 61;
sedimentary rock, 36, 136; talus
slope, 52, 55, 150, 151. *See also*
Arroyo(s); Barranca(s); Bolsón(s);
Cave(s); Desert(s); Erosion;
Limestone; Sótano(s); Volcanism
Gold, 29, 162
Gómez Farías, 84, 103, 104; birds of, *95*,
100
Grass(es), *76*, 156, 164; bluestem, 27;
cattail (*Typha domingensis*), *78-79*;
chino grama (*Bouteloua ramosa*), 27,
50-51; needle- (*Stipa tenuissima*), *30*;
side-oats grama, 27; tobosa, 27
Grasslands, *12-13*, 36, 118, 120
Grusonia (*Grusonia bradtiana*), *80*, 82
Gruta del Palmito, 52-59
Gum, sweet (*Liquidambar styraciflua*),
64, 104, *108-109*, 112
Gypsum, 70; crystals, 70, 71; flats, 68-
69. *See also* Dune(s)

H

Harms, Bob, 100, 101, 102, 103
Harms, Sirpa, 100, 103
Harrison, John William Francis, 85, 90
Hawk(s): red-tailed, 20; roadside
(*Buteo magnirostris*), *100*, 103
Hickory, shagbark (*Carya ovata*), *105*
Horgan, Paul, quoted, 20
Humboldt butterfly bush (*Buddleia
humboldtiana*), *108-109*
Hummingbird(s), 67, 166; violet-
crowned (*Amazilia violiceps*), 168

I

Indian(s): Apache, 29; artifacts, 34, 41,
128-129, 132-133; Aztec, *86*, 87;
Chichimec, 125-126, 129, 132; Chisos,

29; Comanche, 29, 31; Huastec, 64;
Tarahumara, 127, 154, *156-157,
158-159*, 160, 165
Indian Springs, *98*, 100

J

Jay(s): green (*Cyanocorax yncas*), *95*;
Mexican, 33, 135
Juniper(s), 119, 128; alligator, 34;
drooping, 33

L

La Joya de Sala, 93, 96, 99
Ladies' tresses (*Spiranthes polyantha*),
175
Laguna Grande, 70, *74-75*
Laguna de Guzman, *96-97*, 136, *140-141*
Laguna de los Mexicanos, 96, 99
Laurel(s), sweet (*Illicium floridanum*),
114
Legler, John M., 75
Limestone, 16, 22, *37, 62-63*, 85, 93, *98*,
101, *116-117*; boulders, 36, *46-47*, 100;
erosion, *38-39*, 66; porosity, 85, 106
Lizard(s), 121; alligator (*Gerrhonotus
liocephalus*), *77*; spiny, 34
Louteridium (*Louteridium
tamaulipense*), *114*
Lumholtz, Carl, 125-126; photographs
by, *156-157, 158-159*

M

McKitrick, Mary, 92, 94
Mala mujer (*Cnidoscolus urens*), *60, 66,
108-109*, 166
Malachite, *89*
Mancinas, Vicente, 151, 152, 154, 156,
162, 164, 165
Manzanita, *122-123*
Maple, Mexican sugar (*Acer skutchii*),
108, *112*
Mariscal Canyon, 28
Marsh, E. G., Jr., 75
Marshes, 68, 70, 93, 96
Mesquite, 22, 36, (*Prosopis glandulosa*),
42, 54, *70, 72, 73, 140-141*, 152, 158
Milkwort (*Polygala turgida*), 76, *77*
Minckley, W. L., 75
Moctezuma (Aztec ruler), *86*, 87
Moonpod bush (*Selinocarpus
purpusiana*), *71*

Moss, club, *98*
Munn, Charles, III, 92, 93, 94, 96

N

Nolina nelsonii, 116-117

O

Oak(s), 32, 64, 82, 93, 104, *108-109, 116-
117*, 118, 120, *122-123*
Ocotillo (*Fouquieria splendens*), 20, 22,
54, *68-69*
Orchid(s), 104, 108, 116, 166; clamshell
(*Epidendrum cochleatum*), *111*; crybe
(*Crybe rosea*), *111*; govenia (*Govenia
liliacea*), *111*; hyacinth (*Arpophyllum
spicatum*), *111*; malaxis (*Malaxis
corymbosa*), *111*; serpent head
(*Stanhopea devoniensis*), *110-111*
Oriole, Altimira, or Lichtenstein's
oriole (*Icterus gularis*), *95*

P

Palm(s), fan (Brahea moorei), 105
Paper flower(s), (*Psilostrophe
tagetina*), 36, *50-51*
Parakeet(s), green (*Aratinga holo-
chlora*), 60, 61, *62-63*, 65
Parrot(s), 87, 103, 126
Phelan, Dick, 119, 124, 125
Pine(s), *116-117*, 118, 120, *122-123*, 128,
150, *166-167*; piñon, 34; ponderosa, 32.
See also Forest(s)
Pine(s), marsh, 74, 75
Podocarpus (*Podocarpus reichii*), 108,
112
Poinsettia, wild (*Euphorbia
cyathophora*), *115*
Posos Bonitos, 76, *78-79*
Pulliam Peak, 29
Pyrrhuloxia (*Pyrrhuloxia sinuata*), *94-
95*, 96

Q

Quetzal. *See* Trogon

R

Ralph, Ron, 57-58, 61
Rancho del Cielo, 84-85, 87, 90,
104; birdwatching at, 88-89,
91-103
Reddell, James, 59

Reeds, carrizo (Arundo donax), 44-45
Río Bravo. See Río Grande
Río Casas Grandes, 136, 139, 140
Río Churince, 76
Río Conchos, 36
Río Frio, 106
Río Grande, 20, 24-25, 36, 37, 43, 44-45, 50-51
Río Hondo, 164
Río el Naranjo, end papers 2-3
Río Sabinas, 106-107
Río Urique, 150, 153, 154-156, 160, 161, 162-164
Río Verde, 166

S

Salt cedar, 36, 48
Saltbush (Atriplex canescens), 70
Salvatierra, Padre Juan Maria, quoted, 148
San Luis Potosí, 8
San Marcos Mountains, 68
Sand: canyon beaches, 44, 155; formation of, 44, 139. See also Dune(s)
Sandoval Loera, Ingeniero Efrain, 150, 151
Santa Elena Canyon, 35, 36-51; early explorers, 28
Scarlet runner bean (Phaseolus coccineus), 108-109
Scorpion(s), 24; Vejovis coahuilae, 78
Sedge(s), 76
Selenite crystals, 73
Seneca, quoted, 52
Sierra del Carmen, 31, 35
Sierra de Guatemala, 84, 85, 104; birds of, 88
Sierra Madre: early explorers, 87; name origin, 24
Sierra Madre Occidental, cover, end

paper 4-page 1, 16, 21, 166; barranca country, 149; exploration and settlement, 124, 125, 126, 132, 156; highlands, 163; volcanic origins, 16, 22
Sierra Madre Oriental, end papers 2-3, 21, 31, 84, 104; basins, 68, 136; caves, 52-54; limestone geology, 16, 22, 54, 60; rivers, 36
Sierra Madre del Sur, 24
Sierra de la Nariz, 142-143
Sierra del Nido, 119-135; forests, 122-123
Sierra del Presidio, 144
Sierra Ponce, 38-39
Sierra de Samalayuca, 144, 146-147
Sierra de San Marcos, 68
Snake(s), 24, 34; black-tailed rattler (Crotalus molossus), 32; Willard's rattler, 121
Sótano(s), 22, 54, 61, 65, 66
Sótano de las Golondrinas, 60-65
Sotol(s) (Dasylirion cedrosanum), 81
Spider(s): crab, 69; tarantula, 24; wolf, 71
Spring(s): limestone, 61, 98; thermal, 68, 70, 78, 152
Spurge, gypsum (Euphorbia fruticulosa), 73
Sutton, George Miksch, 102

T

Tagetes (Tagetes lucida), 115
Thistle(s), 77
Tiger apple (Tigridia pavonia), 115
Traven, B., quoted, 118
Trinity plant(s) (Thevetia peruviana), 114
Trogon(s), 87; mountain, 86, 87; quetzal, 101
Turk's cap (Malvaviscus arboreus), 114

Turtle(s), box (Terrapene coahuilae), 74, 75

V

Vegetation: biotic province of Sierra Madre, 21, 22, 84, 104; drought-resistant, 26, 27, 42, 161; epiphytes, 108, 110-111, 113, 116; introduced species, 85, 156; parasitic, 113; poisonous, 60, 66; root systems, 72, 73, 139, 176, 177; spines, 24, 69, 134.
Vine(s), 106; love, 113
Volcanism: ash, 118; and geology of Occidental, 16, 22; lava, 118; lava field, 8-9; rhyolite, 136, 138-139; rock, 136, 149, 166, 173; terrain, 10-11; volcanoes, 24

W

Warburton, Barbara, 85, 90, 91, 92, 93, 100
Weather: drought, 145; flooding, 36, 44, 82; fog, 124; seasonal variation, 21, 27, 36, 96, 108, 161, 166; rainbow, end paper 4-page 1; summer cloudburst, 144; temperature shifts, 124
Webster, Frank, 85, 90
Wedelia (Wedelia hispida), 116-117
Wendt, Tom, 68, 71, 74
Whetten, Nathan, 22
Woodpecker(s): acorn, 102, 135; Campephilus imperialis, 126

Y

Yucca(s), 22, 54; beaked, 2-3; Spanish dagger (Yucca treculeana), 70, 73, 130; Torrey (Yucca torreyi), 40-41

Z

Zephyranthes (Zephyranthes clintiae), 114, 115